THE
SHAAR
PRESS

THE JUDAICA IMPRINT
FOR THOUGHTFUL PEOPLE

SUC

RELATION

A
SHAAR
PRESS
PUBLICATION

RABBI ABRAHAM J. TWERSKI, M.D.

CESSFUL

SHIPS

at Home, at Work and with Friends

Bringing control issues under control

Published by **SHAAR PRESS**
Distributed by MESORAH PUBLICATIONS, LTD.
4401 Second Avenue / Brooklyn, N.Y 11232 / (718) 921-9000

Distributed in Israel by SIFRIATI / A. GITLER
6 Hayarkon Street / Bnei Brak 51127

Distributed in Europe by LEHMANNS
Unit E, Viking Industrial Park, Rolling Mill Road / Jarrow, Tyne and Wear, NE32 3DP/ England

Distributed in Australia and New Zealand by GOLDS WORLD OF JUDAICA
3-13 William Street / Balaclava, Melbourne 3183 / Victoria Australia

Distributed in South Africa by KOLLEL BOOKSHOP
Shop 8A Norwood Hypermarket / Norwood 2196, Johannesburg, South Africa

ISBN: 1-57819-348-6 Hard Cover
ISBN: 1-57819-349-4 Paperback

Printed in the United States of America by Noble Book Press
Custom bound by Sefercraft, Inc. / 4401 Second Avenue / Brooklyn N.Y. 11232

Table of Contents

Introduction

Quite often, we hear the advice, "Take control!" This can indeed be sound advice provided it is understood that the control taken is of *oneself*. Unfortunately, some people are rather lax in self-control, but may exert much effort in trying to control other people.

Controlling others is morally wrong. The Talmud says that whereas G–d controls *everything* in the universe, He does *not* control a person's ethical and moral behavior (*Berachos* 33b). G–d allows people to have free choice to behave as they wish. If relinquishing control is good enough for G–d, Who *does* have the ability to control people's behavior, it should certainly be good enough for human beings who *cannot* control what others do. G–d wishes people to choose to behave properly because they have come to the understanding that such behavior is right. That should be the goal of human beings as well.

The Torah says that if a man steals a person (kidnaps) and sells him, he commits a capital crime (*Exodus* 21:16).The Chazon Ish says that mitzvos of the Torah may have many implications. Referring to this verse, the Chazon Ish says that it implies that one may not "steal" a person's freedom from him. Controlling a person is depriving him of his free choice, and this is analogous to "stealing" him (*MeShulchan Govoha, Shemos* p.145).

Inasmuch as people cannot, in fact, control others, the attempt to control is doomed to failure, resulting in frustration and disappointment. There appears to be an innate drive to resist control, so that whatever might have been achieved by logical conviction is undone by one's attempt to control.

We may *think* that we are in control of something, whereas the facts indicate otherwise. Let us look at a comparison between the control a driver has of his automobile versus the control a driver has of his horse. If one wishes the horse to turn to the right, one tugs on the right rein. This pulls on the bit in the horse's mouth, causing the horse to feel pain. To avoid the pain, the horse turns to the right. One has not actually *controlled* the horse. Rather, one has made it an offer that is difficult to refuse. Theoretically, if the horse was extremely hungry and saw a pile of hay to the left, it is conceivable that the hunger would override the pain and it would turn to the left rather than to the right.

It is different with an automobile. When one turns the steering wheel to the right, the car has no choice. The driver is actually controlling the car.

It is important to distinguish between the two. Sometimes we think we are in control of someone as with an automobile, whereas we are only making defiance of our will so difficult for the person that he chooses to comply. This is an attempt to control *by intimidation*.

The tendency to resist being controlled appears to be innate. The Talmud cites a dispute between R' Yehudah HaNasi and the Roman leader, Antoninus. R' Yehudah held that the *yetzer hara* (evil inclination) enters a person at the moment of conception. Antoninus argued that if this were so, the fetus would kick his way out of the womb, and R' Yehudah conceded (*Sanhedrin* 91b).

R' Avraham Grodzinsky asks, why would the *yetzer hara* cause the fetus to leave the womb to a certain death? What pursuit of pleasure can a fetus possibly have? He answers that the primary drive of the *yetzer hara* is not so much the pursuit of pleasure as the desire to throw off all restrictions. If the fetus had a *yetzer hara,* it would go to its death in the desire to escape the confinement of the womb.

The *yetzer hara* encompasses many of a person's biologic drives. One of these is the refusal to be controlled or confined. From the very moment a person is born with a *yetzer hara,* he resists being controlled.

If you have ever watched a six-month-old infant being fed, this scene will be familiar to you. The mother puts a spoonful of cereal at the infant's mouth, and the baby defiantly clamps his lips shut. The mother tries to distract the child by playing with colored beads or the like. The infant becomes so absorbed with the beads that he opens his mouth a bit. Mother takes prompt advantage of this lapse to push the spoonful of cereal into his mouth.

The child knows he has been had, so he keeps the cereal in his mouth, refusing to swallow it. Again, the mother resorts to distraction, pouring beans from one cup into another. The baby is distracted, and the bolus of food touches the back of his pharynx, triggering the automatic swallowing reflex. The whole procedure is repeated with every spoonful. A feeding which should have taken five minutes may take twenty or more minutes.

You may say, perhaps the infant was just not hungry. Forget it! If the mother goes to answer the telephone and leaves the bowl of cereal within the baby's reach, on her return she may find the child digging into the cereal with both hands, with sticky goo all over his face. The child did want to eat, but was adamant that his mother not control his eating.

Because the infant must eat, he loses this round of his struggle for independence. But soon another battleground is encountered.

Mother wishes to toilet-train him, and here he really shows her that he cannot be manipulated. Mother may perform all kinds of suggestive maneuvers to convey the message to the child, but he stares at her with his big blue eyes with a look that seems to say, "I haven't the faintest idea what you want of me." But no sooner is his diaper replaced, than he does what mother wanted done elsewhere. The message is loud and clear (if we only listen): "I refuse to be controlled."

Eventually the child realizes that he is little and unable to get many of the things he wants on his own. His parents are big and capable of giving him what he wants, but they appear to have set a price: He must listen to them. The child then enters into a "negotiated" contract which, although unspoken, is every bit as valid as one drawn up by a team of attorneys. It is essentially this: "I will comply with your wishes so that you will give me the things I cannot get by myself."

The child's obedience and compliance with their wishes make the parents think that they have control of the child. Nothing could be further from the truth. When you pay the grocer for the item he gives you, you are not controlling him at all. It is merely a transaction. That is essentially what much of childhood obedience is: a transaction.

Implicit in this transaction, at least in the child's mind, is, "And when I am big enough to get many of the things I want without my parents' help, the deal is off. I will no longer have to pay for my wants by complying with their wishes."

As the child grows older, his behavior may take a radical turn. The parents are bewildered. "What has happened with our son? What's gotten into him? He was always such an obedient child." Nothing has gotten in to him. It is simply that the parents did not understand the terms of the contract. They had the pleasant delusion that they were able to control the child.

The long and short of it is that control does not work. It may *appear* to work, but this appearance is very deceptive.

This was clearly stated by the Vilna Gaon in his commentary on *Proverbs*. Solomon says, "Train the child according to his way;

when he grows older he will not deviate from it" (*Proverbs* 22:6). The Gaon says that if you try to force the child into something he is not by nature, you may succeed as long as he fears you, but when he grows older, he will revert to his natural inclination. If you go along with the child's natural endowment and channel it in the right direction, he is likely to retain this behavior. If you try to force him to be something he is not, he may comply as long as the pressure is on, but when the pressure is off, he will return to his innate inclination. The Gaon is describing "control by intimidation" and says that it is futile.

There are ways of bringing about desirable behavior, whether it is parents with their children, spouses with each other, teachers with their students or any other relationship. These ways can be learned and implemented, but it must first be accepted that *control does not work*. As long as one thinks he can control by any type of coercion, one is not likely to seek more effective and constructive ways.

I am very concerned that the problem of control has worsened and tends to be progressive in our culture. Why?

When I was a child, I had a little toy car that I had to push to make it go. Later, I had a wind-up car that could go without my pushing it, but I could not control where it would go. Recently, I came into a room where a three-year-old child was sitting on the floor holding a remote-control instrument, gleefully directing the movements of a toy truck that was on the other side of the room. I thought, "How is this child going to learn that there are things he *cannot* control, when at the age of three he can wield such control?"

When Explorer II went into space beyond the solar system, it still responded to an order from Central Command. I felt a tingling in my spine. If we can wield control over something more than *two billion miles* away, how are we going to accept that we cannot control something or someone at our fingertips?

There is only one person whom you can actually control: *yourself*. So be wise and apply control to yourself. For anyone else, try to learn ways to relate which will prove constructive.

Let's Define Control

Control: *The capacity to manage, master, dominate, exercise power over, regulate, influence, curb, suppress, or restrain.*

At the risk of overgeneralizing, I believe it is safe to say that many, if not most, problems in relationships — between husband/wife, parent/child, employer/employee, spiritual leader/congregant, teacher/student and various others — are very often the result of one individual trying to exert control over the other person.

Everyone may have a need to wield control, and there are many relationships which may indeed require a degree of control. Exceeding an acceptable amount of control invites trouble.

An appropriate term for a person who exercises excessive control has been coined by Dr. Les Parrott: *Control Freak*, which is the title of his book on the subject. In addition to my clinical experience, I have drawn upon Dr. Parrott's work and a variety of other sources in writing this book.

It is rather easy to identify others as being "control freaks." Recognizing the control freak in ourselves is far more difficult.

The term "control freak" has a connotation of tyranny or irrationality, and this is not true of many controlling people who may share some of the control freak's traits in a much milder form. Yet, I believe use of the term is justified because although the controlling *person* may not be perceived as a freak, the control per se may be felt as extremely unpleasant.

Dr. Parrott points out that although the word "freak" has a negative clang, it is really not a derogatory term. He says, "Control freaks are people who care more than you do about something and won't stop at being pushy to get their way."

I hope to clarify some concepts about control, give some constructive suggestions how to better relate to control freaks and how to recognize this trait in ourselves. There may be relatively little that we can do to change other people, but there is a great deal we can do to make salutary changes in ourselves.

As with many other conditions, the diagnosis is more than half the cure. If we can identify the control freak in both ourselves and in others, our lives will undoubtedly become much more pleasant.

The Good Kind of Control

We have all experienced, at one time or another, the distressing feeling of "things spinning out of control." It is frightening when we feel helpless, tossed about in a chaotic world over which we have no control. On the other hand, to the degree that we feel we have some control over our lives, to that degree we feel less distressed, if not happier.

The psychiatrist Viktor Frankl describes the dehumanization that occurred to him in the concentration camps. Everything was taken from him, and he was under the ruthless domination of the camp guards. He had no control over anything. However, Frankl says, he had control over his attitude. He had a choice of how he was going to accept death. This was one choice the Nazis could not take from him, and he found strength in having the ability to control his attitude, even if it was only an attitude towards death.

An interesting observation was made of patients in severe pain. Some had to request pain medication from a nurse, while others had an apparatus whereby they could administer their own pain medication. Studies revealed that those patients who could control their own medication used *less* pain medication than those who had to ask the nurse for it. The apparent conclusion is that being in control of oneself and not being helplessly dependent on others may reduce the severity of physical pain and the need for drugs.

Having control over one's attitude may affect one's adjustment to life. At one wedding, when everyone was dancing, a woman with multiple sclerosis who was in a wheelchair drummed with her fingers on the table. "I am dancing, too," she said. "It's just that my feet aren't moving like other people's." It has been demonstrated that one's attitude can have a major effect on the course of illness and recovery.

My work in treating alcoholics and drug addicts has brought me into close contact with people who have lost control of themselves. When the urge to drink or take a drug comes on, they feel compelled to do so. A striking characteristic of these people is that they cannot delay gratification. They are virtually helpless to resist the urge.

Being able to delay gratification allows a person to gain control over himself. If a drug addict could say, "O.K., I feel the need for a drug, but I can wait a day or even several hours," he would be well on the way to recovery. This is one of the key features of the Alcoholics Anonymous program: "Take one day at a time. You don't have to drink today. You can worry about tomorrow tomorrow."

This may be one of the reasons why self-control problems are so common today. Our wonderful technology has eliminated so many of the needs for delay. We have a broad variety of instant foods. We have microwave ovens, fax machines, e-mail, jet planes, high-speed copiers. Many of the things for which we had to wait in the past are available to us immediately. As our tolerance for delay erodes, our ability to exercise self-control diminishes.

To the degree that an individual does not have control over himself, to that degree he is under control of external forces and other people.

The Talmud states it so clearly. "If a person is in a rage, all the forces of hell have control over him" (*Nedarim* 22a). If a person loses control of his anger, something else takes over and controls him.

Just as an addict loses control of himself and is enslaved by alcohol or drugs, so does a person who is a slave to making money, to pursuing acclaim or to any other compelling urge.

In the Haggadah *From Bondage to Freedom,* I pointed out that our daily references to the Exodus are not in commemoration of our political independence, but of our being free of all coercive forces that take away our ability to make proper choices. Our physical body, which is essentially an animal body, makes many demands. Animals are not free, because they cannot resist the dictates of their bodies. We have been given a Torah which enables us to be masters of ourselves rather than slaves to our bodies.

The Torah says that the Ten Commandments were *chorus al haluchos,* inscribed on the Tablets (*Exodus* 32:16). The Sages (*Avos* 6:2) say that inasmuch as there are no vowel signs in the Torah, the Hebrew word *chorus* can also be read as *cherus* (liberty). The Torah is saying that the Word of G–d makes man free. By observing the mitzvos and *middos* prescribed by the Torah, we free ourselves from the tyranny of the body and can achieve self-control. *The essential feature that distinguishes a human being is the ability to have self-control.*

Control and *power* are closely related. Good power is self-mastery. Exerting power over others can be problematic.

There is reason to believe that infants develop the *feeling*, although they are unable to develop the *thought*, that they are all-powerful. This may begin when mothers respond to infants' needs. When the baby cries and mother feeds it, the baby may develop the *feeling* that "my crying brings mother," "my crying brings food" or "I can control my mother by crying." Granted, infants may not be able to conceptualize this, but the *emotion* of being in control may be there. Clinically, we sometimes see adult patients who have residuals of the "magical thinking" that existed in infancy. The idea of "I can make things happen by wanting them" can cause problems. For example, a person who is very angry at someone may harbor the thought, "I wish he were dead." If the object of his anger should die within a short time after this, the person may feel that it was his wish that caused the death, and he may feel guilty for having caused it. Although he may understand logically that his wish could not kill anyone, the primitive emotion says that it can. When emotions conflict with rational thought, it is the emotions that often triumph.

As the child grows, he begins to see that he is not as powerful as he imagined, as he may not be able to get everything he wants. With growth comes the ability to do more things for himself, and the loss of power that he had over his mother as an infant is compensated for by his own power to do more, or in other words, to be *independent*. But it was his *dependency* on his mother and his ability to control her that worked for him at the beginning. Dependence had its advantages, and independence has its advantages. Independence may produce pride, but dependence may sometimes bring comfort. Here we have the rudiments of the dependence/independence conflict that may persist into adulthood and may be the root of many problems in adjusting to people.

For example, a man who has dependency needs may wish to be dependent on his wife, but when he does so, this frustrates his desire to be independent. This frustration may result in his feeling angry, and the anger may be projected onto the wife. On the other hand, if he asserts his independence, this frustrates his dependency needs. Because these conflicts take place in the subconscious mind, the person may have no idea why he is upset, and when seeking reasons for his frustration, he may implicate people in his environment who are in no way responsible for his discomfort.

Infants are often characterized by, "I want what I want when I want it." Maturation requires acceptance of delay in gratifying an impulse.

There is reason to believe that the ability or inability to delay gratification begins in early childhood, and is indicative of how the person will function and adjust to reality. In *Emotional Intelligence*, psychologist Daniel Goleman describes this test. Four-year-old children are offered a marshmallow and are told that they may eat it now. However, if they wait for fifteen minutes until the tester returns, they can have *two* marshmallows to eat. Some children promptly grab the one marshmallow, while others restrain themselves, and when the tester returns, they receive two marshmallows. Follow-up studies of these children in adolescence showed that the ones who restrained themselves were more self-confident, more assertive, better able to concentrate and more efficient at handling difficulties than those who had grabbed the single marshmallow. Early self-mastery augurs well for a more productive adulthood.

Just as self-control is healthy, trying to control other people is generally unhealthy.

There are situations, however, where control of others is necessary. A small child who wrests himself loose from his parent's grasp and runs toward the road must be controlled. Soldiers on the battlefield need the control of the commanding officer who knows best what action is appropriate and what is inappropriate. In court, a lawyer may tell his client, "Stay quiet. Let me do the talking." There are numerous situations where it is prudent to accept control from someone who is better informed and more capable.

What I am addressing in this book is not the good kind of control, but the kind of control that is, in the long run, detrimental to everyone, the controller as well as the controlee. Let us look now as to how the desire to control others may develop and why people who try to wield control may be unaware of this.

Denial of Control

Many people who are control freaks are completely unaware of this. Similarly, many people who are *being controlled* may be unaware of this. Both may suffer from the negative consequences of control, but they cannot change if they are not aware of the situation.

Psychology describes the phenomenon of *denial*. Denial does not mean that a person is denying something in the usual sense of the word "deny." A person who denies may be telling the truth when he denies having done something, or he may be lying. In either case, the person *is aware* that he is denying something. The term "in denial," as used in psychology, refers to a person being *unaware* of some aspect of reality. The person is *not* consciously lying. He will even swear that what he believes is the truth. Somewhere, deep down in the hidden recesses of his subconscious mind, there is an awareness, but since the person has no access to this awareness, it is of no use to him.

Very often, the reason for the unawareness of reality is that this particular aspect of reality is too painful to accept. To protect the person from the distress of knowing this reality, the mind turns off the awareness. Telling a person who is *in denial* of reality that he should recognize what the reality is, is similar to telling a blind person to look at something. He just cannot do it.

Understandably, denial of reality is often very disruptive, because we all have to live in reality.

When I was an intern in medicine, I saw a case of denial which totally amazed me, because at that time I was not aware of psychological defenses.

A woman was admitted to the hospital for exploratory surgery. She told the doctor that he must be completely frank and truthful with her and not try to protect her feelings. The operation revealed that the woman had cancer, and the doctor told her so. He told her that she would have to undergo chemotherapy.

The chemotherapy had to be administered intravenously, and because the woman had poor surface veins, it required several jabs before the medication could be injected. One time, I gave her the injection. I found a small vein on the back of her hand, and did not have to jab her a second time. She concluded that I was the only doctor she would allow to inject her.

I used to work every Sunday, and every Sunday this woman would come to the hospital, saying, "I'm here for my cancer treatment." Several times she remarked how fortunate she was that she was living in an era of scientific progress, when there was a treatment for cancer. She volunteered to talk to other women who had cancer.

After a number of months, the chemotherapy was no longer effective and she began to experience symptoms caused by the spread of the disease. When she was admitted to the hospital, she said to me angrily, "I can't understand what it is with you doctors. I've been coming to the hospital regularly and no one has been able to find out what's wrong with me."

I was perplexed by her remark. It was as though she had never heard the word "cancer" before. It was only after I studied psychology that I understood what had happened. As long as she was free of symptoms, the word "cancer" was an abstraction, an intellectual concept which did not effect her emotionally. This intellectual concept was not life-threatening, and she could deal with it. When she began feeling the effects of the disease, its life-threatening character was more than she could handle. The anxiety of having cancer was so overwhelming that to protect her, her mind simply shut off her awareness of it.

In my experience with treating alcohol addiction, I have found that denial is virtually always present. A person's life may be falling apart due to his drinking. He is in danger of losing his family, his job, his friends, his driver's license and everything he holds dear, but he steadfastly insists that he does not have a problem with alcohol and does not have to give up drinking. To this person, alcohol is the only thing that makes him feel comfortable, and to recognize that alcohol is the cause of all his troubles would mean that he has to stop drinking. This is so anxiety-provoking to him that his mind simply blocks off what is evident to everyone else. He becomes "blind," as it were, to alcohol being the problem. You can argue with a blind person endlessly, but you cannot make him see.

Denial may also occur in people who are dieting to lose weight but continue to gain weight. They may swear that they had only a half-grapefruit and cottage cheese for breakfast, a salad with low-calorie dressing for lunch, and broiled chicken for dinner. *There is no way one could gain weight on this diet.* They are not lying. They are "in denial" and are actually unaware of the snacks they have during the day.

Who is capable of denial? Everyone. What about highly intelligent people? They are even *more* prone to denial than people of lesser intellect.

The Rabbi of Gur made a penetrating comment on a verse in the Torah. The Torah relates that when the Matriarch Sarah was told that she would bear a child at the age of ninety, she laughed "inwardly," thinking, "How can I bear a child at my old age?" G–d then said to Abraham, "Why did Sarah laugh? Is there anything that is beyond G–d?" Abraham reprimanded Sarah, but "Sarah denied, saying 'I did not laugh' because she feared." Abraham then said to her, "No, you did laugh" (*Genesis* 18:12-14).

The Rabbi of Gur says that it is impossible to think that Sarah lied. The Midrash tells us that Sarah was totally free of sin (*Bereishis Rabbah* 58:1). He, therefore, interprets the word *vayechaches* as meaning not that Sarah *denied*, but that Sarah was *in denial*. Her disbelief that she could carry a child was *bekirbah*, "inward," deep in the recesses of her subconscious. Sarah was not even aware of this thought. Only G–d, Who knows a person's innermost thoughts and feelings, was aware of it. When Abraham reprimanded her for this thought, Sarah could not even conceive that she could have harbored disbelief of G–d's omnipotence. Her reverence of G–d was so great that a thought such as this was beyond her. The verse thus reads, "Sarah was *in denial* because she was so G–d-fearing." Sarah was certain that she was speaking the truth when she said, "I did not laugh." Sarah did not deny or lie. She had no access to her subconscious.

It is not a sin to be in denial. G–d's reprimand was that Sarah's trust in Him should have been so profound that it should have prevented even a subconscious thought.

Given the understanding of denial as being a defense mechanism which is beyond our awareness, we can understand how even great people may be in denial.

A control freak may feel that being in control of others is as vital to him as alcohol is to the alcoholic. He may not be able to see that this is a behavior that he must relinquish. A person who is being controlled by others may not be able to see this because it might threaten a relationship upon which he is dependent, or because it might be a blow to his ego. An example of this is a husband who cannot see that he is being controlled by his wife. This realization would be demeaning, and it might call for him to react to her control in a way that might disrupt their relationship upon which he is dependent. Similarly, a wife who is controlled by her husband may be in denial of this and even of his abusiveness, because to acknowledge it might mean that their relationship is in jeopardy, and this is too threatening a thought for her.

Low self-esteem is often responsible for the denial. If a control freak had better self-esteem, he would not be threatened by relinquishing control. If the subject of control had better self-esteem, he would not feel his ego was offended and would be more secure so that the threat of losing his dependency would not be overwhelming.

In alcoholism, it may take a major crisis to break through the alcoholic's denial. It is as if the crisis overcomes the "blindness" and enables a "blind" person to see. In control, it may also require some kind of crisis to make a person realize that he is a control freak or the subject of a controlling person. Just as in alcoholism we make every effort to overcome the denial without a major crisis, so too when dealing with control. It is possible that a deeper understanding of all that control involves may enable a person to gain better insight of his behavior; he may make the requisite character changes to relinquish control or to deal more effectively with controlling people.

While on the subject of denial, I feel it is important to be aware of a very dangerous type of denial, and that is when parents are in denial of a child's problems. The thought that a child may have a learning disability or an emotional disorder can be so threatening to parents that they are rendered incapable of seeing it. This is particularly dangerous because if a problem is not detected and addressed early, the complications that may arise as a child develops can be very destructive, whereas early detection can often forestall such consequences.

A fifteen-year-old girl was away from home, attending high-school in another city. The couple with whom she roomed suspected that she was bulimic, bingeing on food and purging herself.

They informed the principal, who called the parents. The parents said this was impossible and that the couple was in error. The bulimic symptoms increased in severity, and when the principal told the parents that the young woman needed help, they withdrew her from the school and placed her in a different school. They were very angry that the principal had dared to "accuse" their daughter of being bulimic.

Some adolescents who are admitted for treatment had been using drugs for several years. The parents did not "choose" to ignore this. Rather, they were in denial. When things were missing from the home, they could not think it possible that their son had taken them to sell for money to buy drugs. Such denial delays treatment.

I have seen cases where parents were simply incapable of being aware that their eleven-year-old child was unable to read, or that an adolescent had a mood disorder. If they do notice that something is not alright, their attitude is "he/she will outgrow it." In older adolescents their attitude may be "when he/she gets married, everything will be alright," as if marriage is a hospital. Problems that could be resolved are neglected and may lead to additional adjustment problems. When matters reach a crisis point and the problem is acknowledged, some of the damage cannot be undone. Young people whose personality problems were expected to be solved by marriage may end up in unhappy marriages which may not survive. In these cases, children of these marriages may come into the world with two strikes against them.

There is no immunity to personality problems. Many of these can be ameliorated significantly with proper help but may only follow a negative progression if neglected.

The Urge to Control

Why do some people have a need to be controlling? I believe that one major reason is that it gives them a feeling of superiority. Why do they need to feel superior? Often it is in order to compensate for their feelings of *inferiority*.

In *Angels Don't Leave Footprints* and *Life's Too Short*, I postulated that many psychological and emotional problems are rooted in low self-esteem, in an *unwarranted* sense of unworthiness and/or incompetence. I described a number of behavior patterns that are a result of a person's trying to cope with or escape from these painful feelings.

There is a Yiddish aphorism, "What makes a small child happy? Seeing a child who is smaller than himself." Surrounded by seemingly gigantic adults, a small child may feel insignificant. If he sees a child smaller than himself, the awareness that he is bigger than someone else is very pleasant.

This is as true of adults as it is of children. People with low self-esteem who feel small may try to bolster their sagging self-esteem by associating with people to whom they can feel superior. They may try to further enhance their self-esteem by dominating their subordinates. The Talmud wisely says, "Be a tail to lions rather than a leader of foxes" (*Ethics of the Fathers* 4:20). A person with good self-esteem does not have a need to be "a leader of foxes." He is comfortable associating with "lions," albeit in a subordinate position, because he can learn much from them. The leader of foxes rarely grows, because he does not allow himself to learn from subordinates. A person who does not wish to associate with wise and competent people (lions) and chooses to associate with less wise and less competent people (foxes) because he can be their leader is what Dr. Parrott so appropriately calls a "control freak."

I recall having grade school teachers whom I loved. They were kind and caring, and just thrilled to teach and to see their students grow. But I also remember a fourth-grade teacher who was mean. She was a despot, and she tyrannized us kids. She had absolute rule over us and gloated over it. We all disliked her, and the more assertive of us would do things to irritate and provoke her. In retrospect I feel rather sorry for her, because the only way she could obtain a sense of worthiness and competence was by dominating ten-year-olds.

I once saw a young psychiatric resident approach the chief of the institute with a question. The latter screamed at him, "Don't you know protocol!" He was supposed to ask the chief's secretary for an appointment to speak to the great one. How dare he approach him directly! I felt sorry for the chief, whose psychiatric insights had not elevated his self-esteem.

When I worked in a state mental hospital, there were attendants who empathized with the mentally ill and cared for them. But there were some who basked in their position of authority, exercising it over people who had no recourse.

I shall never forget an experience during my first year of training in psychiatry. I was walking down the corridor of a unit in the psychiatric hospital, and I was jingling my keys. One patient said to me, "You have the keys to the door and I don't. You can leave when you want to and I can't. You don't have to remind me of it." I shall be forever grateful to that patient who put me in my place. I had no idea that by jingling my keys I was demeaning her while flaunting my authority.

Our greatest leaders in history did not seek positions of authority but were pushed into them. I am not referring to rulers who conquered other countries, but to truly great personalities who were humbled by their position of leadership rather than inflated by it. The outstanding example is, of course, Moses. "Who am I that I should go to Pharaoh?" (*Exodus* 3:11). He was reluctant to assume the leadership of Israel, and when he did, he remained "the most humble of all men on earth" (*Numbers* 12:3). Perhaps second only to Moses was Hillel, who was catapulted into the position of leadership, and whose humility is legendary. Leaders must exercise their authority, but they do so in consideration and for the betterment of their subjects and followers, rather than to feed their grandiosity.

A not uncommon problem in family life is abuse of spouse and children. How sick a person must be in order to abuse little children! A husband who manipulates things so that he can dominate his wife is also betraying how little he thinks of himself.

There are a variety of ways of abusing a spouse or children, and they all have the same cause: *the need to control.*

I know of wealthy people who exerted control over their family members. The latter wanted to remain in their good graces and not defy them, lest they forfeit their gifts or bequests. These people lived in fear of their father, grandfather or uncle, but did not dare to defy his wishes lest they be written out of the will. They complied with the "old man's" wishes with reluctance, and their feelings were of resentment rather than love. They could hardly wait for the time when "Dear Uncle" would pass on so that they could share in the inheritance and no longer have to cater to his idiosyncrasies.

Control breeds resentment, not love.

If you are in a position of authority, whether in the family, occupationally or socially, handle it delicately. You will get far better results and be loved as well as respected.

Closely related to the lack of self-esteem is what one psychologist calls "disconnection." As we will see later, some people do not develop an inner identity. They are what others expect them to be. Having no true "self" with which one can be connected, one reaches out in desperation to "connect" with someone else. This connection can be either by controlling others or allowing oneself to be controlled by others (*Controlling People,* Patricia Evans). Dr. Parrott feels that controlling people may be ridden with anxiety. "Control freaks are grabbing for anything and anybody that will keep them afloat as their personal anxiety rises."

The need to control may actually begin in childhood. If a child does not develop a sense of trust in others, he may feel that the only security he can have is being in control of things himself. This feeling can grow with him as he matures. The child may develop the feeling that, "If you don't control others, they will control you."

It is not unusual for a person to feel much more secure behind the wheel of the automobile than when in the passenger seat. Although the driver may be competent, the passenger may worry about whether he may have to make a short stop and possibly rear-end the car in front of him or be rear-ended. Is he cautious enough about changing lanes? Will he be able to get back into the right lane after passing before he meets an oncoming car? Is he driving too closely to the parked cars? These concerns do not bother you when you are the driver because you are in control. You are not nearly as secure when you are the passenger and do not have control. Of course, the greater your trust in the driver, the greater your security and the less your anxiety.

The basis of trust begins in childhood, when a child learns that he can trust his parents. If his parents do not relate to him in a trustworthy manner, the child may lack the rudiments of trust. Of course, even if a person does develop trust, it is possible that traumatic events may shake his trust, particularly if his expectations result in disappointment or if he finds his world to be unpredictable. Adults who were abused in childhood by a person whom they trusted may have great difficulty in building relationships. Attempts to rebuild trust may not succeed, as one may maintain underlying fear and suspicion.

We can see this clearly in the generation of the Exodus. Moses repeatedly reminds the Israelites of the great miracles they saw with their own eyes and the voice of G–d which they heard with their own ears, yet they continued to doubt G–d and failed to trust Him.

Can we not but wonder how it was possible for the Israelites not to have complete trust in G–d? Having witnessed the miraculous deliverance from Egypt and the dividing of the Reed Sea, the daily provision of the manna whose excess spoiled overnight except for Shabbos when it remained fresh for two days, the emergence of water from a rock, the Clouds of Glory that encircled and protected them, the Pillar of Fire which illuminated and guided them to travel in the darkness of night—how is it possible that they did not have faith and trust in G–d? Moses pointed out to them that they lacked the trust that G–d would enable them to conquer Canaan, although, "You saw in the desert how G–d carried you as a father carries his child…and in this thing [the conquest of Canaan] you do not have faith in G–d" (1:31-32). How could they deny the evidence of their own senses?

The answer can only be that in the decades of torture and dehumanization in their enslavement in Egypt, never knowing where or when the next cruel attack upon them would be coming, whatever sense of trust they may have had was destroyed. Although they initially responded to Moses' promise of emancipation, they quickly relapsed into distrust (*Exodus* 5:21). It took Moses forty years of teaching to instill trust in a new generation. Shortly before his death he said, "G–d did not give you a heart to know, eyes to see and ears to hear until this day" (*Deuteronomy* 29:3). It was only after forty years of his teaching and the repetitious times that they expressed their needs and were provided with them that they were able to accept the testimony of their eyes and ears.

The Torah gives us important guidelines for developing trust in children. It was the lack of awareness of this important concept that resulted in the debacle of permissiveness which taught that children should be spared from all stress. *If parents anticipate all their child's needs and provide for them before the child has had an opportunity to identify the need, the child may never learn that his needs will be met.* A child must be allowed to feel his needs, and when the parents respond in a way that meets those needs, that is when the child learns to trust.

This is stated so beautifully and clearly in the Torah. Moses says, "*He stressed you and hungered you, and fed you the manna*...so that you should know that a person does not live by bread alone, but by all the utterances of G–d does a person live" (ibid. 8:3). Had G–d provided the manna *before* they were hungry, they never would have been able to learn trust in Him.

Of course, if parents do not understand the child's needs or allow too long a period of frustration, the child does not learn trust either. And when the child lacks the security of being able to trust, he feels he must take things into his own hands, i.e., *control.* Good parenting requires that we walk a fine line between allowing a child to feel his needs and responding to them within a reasonable amount of time so that the child knows that his parents understand, care and provide for him. This will decrease one factor that breeds control.

Needless to say, if a child is abused or shamed by parents or teachers, he may lose trust. If he feels unable to rely on parents and teachers, he learns to trust only himself and to be in cautious control of his environment. The shattering of his trust and security may also render him anxious and suspicious of everyone and everything in his environment.

All this notwithstanding, it is possible that even with the finest parenting and the most sensitive teachers, a child may nevertheless develop a need to control. Why?

Take note of this experiment.

Infants of *eight weeks* were provided with an air pillow. Pressure of the head on the pillow turned on a switch that was connected to a mobile of brightly colored balls that was suspended over the crib. Pressure on the pillow caused the mobile to turn. Another group of eight-week-old infants had a similar pillow and mobile, but the pillow was not connected to the mobile, so that pressure on the pillow did nothing.

Believe it or not, the group of infants whose pillow-pressure caused the mobile to turn apparently learned *at eight weeks* that pressing their heads on the pillow caused the mobile to turn, because they greatly increased the number of times they pressed the pillow. The other group of infants did not!

By the way, the infants in the first group were smiling and cooing after three days, whereas the other infants were not. Apparently there is something very pleasant about being in control, in this case being able to control the mobile with pressing the head against the pillow. [*Helplessness,* Martin Seligman, 46.]

If tiny infants can get pleasure out of control, just think how much more so this holds true as the child matures. It is well established that pleasurable activities are repeated. This may be a reason why even children who developed trust in their parents may become "controllers." *Control may produce pleasure*, and the human body is prone to pursue anything that produces pleasure.

The trait of being a controller or being controlled may simply be due to the way a child grew up. If in his home one parent controlled the other, the child may identify with either parent and take on that parent's character traits. In this case it is not as much a *need* to control or to be controlled as it is the only way a child learned to behave. There may be reasons why the child identified with one parent rather than the other, but the development of the controlling/being controlled behavior is much like the development of style of talking or walking. The child simply mimics the parent's behavior.

Attempting to control for whatever reason, whether for pleasure seeking, to boost one's self-esteem or mimicking a parent, is most unwise. Let us see why.

The Folly of Control

The more we understand about control, the more we will realize how foolish it is to try to control other people.

Remember how you "control" a horse? By pulling on the rein in order to cause it pain. To escape the pain, the horse turns in the direction you desire. This is "control by intimidation." In the days of slavery, a master exercised control by intimidation, because slaves were at his mercy. *If you are in a position of authority or superiority which enables you to control by intimidation, your attempts to control are insulting and demeaning because you are essentially treating the other person as a horse, and you are insulting and demeaning yourself by becoming a cruel taskmaster.* The person whom you are attempting to control may fear you, but will hardly love you. If you think that being a taskmaster elevates your self-esteem, you are seriously mistaken. Keep this golden rule in mind: Except for specific sports activities where it is the point of the game, *you can't build yourself up by knocking someone else down!*

Inasmuch as actual control of another person is impossible, trying to control is counterproductive. Let me share a personal incident that illustrates this.

The shortest way from my home to the hospital was via a steep hill. In winter, when the hill was icy, police put up barricades. On winter mornings, I would drive by the hill, and if the barricades were up, I would use an alternate route.

One morning, seeing that there were no barricades, I assumed the hill was safe. It was not, and the car began to slide down. At the bottom of the hill was a very busy thoroughfare, and I knew I was doomed. There was no way to avoid getting killed. I pumped wildly on the brakes, but it did no good. I tried to steer into the curb to stop, but to no avail. The car was totally out of control. Inasmuch as G–d, for some reason, wanted me to live, I miraculously slid across the thoroughfare without getting hit.

I had no reason to expect a miracle to save my life. If I had been thinking clearly, I would have opened the door and jumped from the car. I most probably would have broken an arm or a leg, but I would live. Staying in the car was certain death. Why did I not jump out? *Because I was still trying to control the car* by pumping on the brakes and turning a non-functioning steering wheel. Had I accepted that the car was out of control, I would have done the logical thing. But no, I persisted in trying to control the uncontrollable, and only a miracle saved my life.

If we realize that other people are uncontrollable, except by intimidation (like a horse), we can use our intellect to find a better way to accomplish what we want. By trying to control the uncontrollable, we are diverted from logical thought, and that is invariably counterproductive.

The more we think we can control things, the harder it is to realize that there are things we cannot control. Let me give you an example.

A major problem of an alcoholic is that he has the delusion that he can control his drinking. His life may be in shambles due to his drinking: his marriage is failing, he is losing his job, his health is impaired and he has been abandoned by his friends. Everyone repeatedly tells him that his drinking is destroying him, but he rejects the obvious because he is adamant that he can control his drinking. Only some kind of crisis can bring him to his senses.

I wrote a book titled *Substance Abusing High Achievers*, describing alcoholism among doctors, CEO's, lawyers and various professionals. These people are particularly resistive to the realization that they cannot control their drinking because they wield control in their occupations. Only a very severe crisis can overcome their delusion.

One patient of mine was a baseball pitcher who had an awesome fastball. He pitched his team to three World Series. However, his drinking had gotten out of hand and was ruining his pitching. His manager and friends pleaded with him to get help for his drinking. He thought they were crazy. Why, he could throw a ball at 103 miles per hour, and had such perfect control that he could get it within a millimeter of where he wanted it to go. How could anyone with such perfect control not have control over alcohol? That was absurd!

After losing a brilliant sports career, he became an insurance salesman, and was soon threatened with being fired because of his drinking. He had to get hit harder before he finally accepted that he had no control over alcohol.

A famous surgeon was told by several colleagues that he drank too much. He was chief of the department of surgery of a major hospital, and his position of authority in which he exercised control made it very difficult for him to accept that he had no control over alcohol. Drunk driving arrests did not convince him that he had an alcohol problem. This realization came only after his car went over an embankment and he had a narrow escape from death.

We thus have a paradox. People who have little control over anything may wish to assert themselves and try to control their spouse and children. People who have much control over some things may be unable to accept that they cannot control other people. Both are likely to be "control freaks." We can see why the problem of control is so ubiquitous.

If only good judgment would prevail! My pitcher patient could have gone on for several more brilliant years as a star athlete. "High-achievers" could avoid the disasters of crises. All "control freaks" could be happier and more productive if they would only accept the truth and desist from trying to control the uncontrollable.

Spare the Rod?

Whenever parents or teachers are criticized for hitting children, two refrains are mentioned in defense of this practice: (1) This was the accepted practice for many centuries, and it produced children who respected their parents and who led Torah-observant lives, and (2) The Torah says "He who spares the whip hates his child" (*Proverbs* 13:24).

R' Shlomo Wolbe states that "*Halachah* is the law that tells us *what* we must do; *mussar* teaches us *how* we must do it." He goes on to say that "changes in times and circumstances may necessitate changes in how we do things." In other words, whereas *halachah* never changes, the way we act within the framework of *halachah* may change (*Alei Shur* vol.1 p.87).

Conditions in Western civilization today are radically different than they were in the *shtetl* (village). Even there, the breakaway *haskalah* movement may have been fueled by the resentment that people had against the beatings by their teachers and by the system that condoned it. However, the environment in the *shtetl* was such that many youngsters remained faithful to Yiddishkeit because *they had nowhere to go if they left it.*

This is no longer the case today. Any youngster who is displeased with the educational system knows that there is a community in the streets that sympathizes with him and is ready to welcome him with open arms.

My work in treating drug addicts has brought me in contact with many of the yeshivah dropouts. Some of these young people ascribe at least part of their rebellion against Yiddishkeit to mistreatment — of themselves and/or their peers — at the hands of parents and teachers, and their perception that it was condoned by the establishment. Today, a teacher who hits a child should know that he may be driving him away from Yiddishkeit and into the ranks of the disaffected.

R' Moshe Leib of Sassov saw that the driver of his coach was whipping the horses. He said to him, "If you knew how to communicate with the horse, you would not need to whip him. Is it fair to whip the horse because of your ignorance?'

If a teacher knew how to communicate with his students, he would never have to resort to physical punishment. Is it fair for a child to be hit because of the teacher's ignorance? A teacher who resorts to hitting a child does not know the first thing about managing a class and does not belong in that position.

As far as the quote from *Proverbs* is concerned, we must understand that what the Torah says is subject to the interpretation of the Talmud and sages. The Karaites could justify eating a cheeseburger because it does not violate the words of the Scripture: "You shall not cook a kid in its mother's milk."

R' Samson Raphael Hirsch translates the verse in *Proverbs* 13:24 as, "He who abstains from *chastisement* hates his child, but he who loves him disciplines him diligently." He does not translate *shevet* to mean "a whip." Solomon is not advocating beating a child.

R' Shlomo Wolbe echoes this interpretation. "There are many ways to chastise. A stern look, an appearance of disappointment — these, too, are a 'whip.' The end of the verse confirms this. *Mussar*, discipline, is what enters the heart of the child (Beatings do not enter a child's heart)...

"Furthermore, we find the prophet saying, 'I took for myself two rods. One I called *pleasant*, and one I called *bruising*' (*Zachariah* 11:7). You can see that there is such a thing as a 'pleasant rod.' This, too, is included in Solomon's words, 'He who abstains from the rod hates his child.' A person can chastise his son with a 'pleasant rod' even more successfully than with a 'bruising rod.'

"And what is the 'pleasant rod' of training? Keep this rule in mind: Encouragement is of greater influence than punishment. A sign of praise or a reward accomplishes more than threats or punishment" (*Alei Shur* vol.1 p.261).

R' Wolbe cites the comment of the Vilna Gaon on the verse quoted earlier, "Train the child according to his way; when he grows older he will not deviate from it" (*Proverbs* 22:6) and elaborates on it.

"You cannot go against a child's natural makeup....*This requires that a father understand what each child's nature is*, because it is impossible to train all the children according to a single formula" (ibid).

Knowing the nature of one's children is the theme of an essay by the ethicist, R' Yerucham Levovitz. R' Yerucham calls our attention to the messages that the Patriarch Jacob gave his sons before his death (*Genesis* 49). These are followed by the verse, "All these are the tribes of Israel—twelve—and this is what their father spoke to them and he blessed them; he blessed each *according to his appropriate blessing*" (ibid. 49:28). However, if we read Jacob's words carefully, we do not find many manifest blessings at all. In fact, we find some reprimand and rebuke (ibid. 49:3-7).

Rashi comments on the words "he blessed each according to his appropriate blessing": "The blessing that was destined to come to each one." R' Yerucham said that in his messages Jacob was essentially describing the *nature* of each son. *If they would each develop and maximize their particular nature, that would be their greatest blessing (Daas Chochmah U'Mussar,* vol. 4 pp. 339-343).

To continue with R' Wolbe's insights, "Just as it is impossible to break a child's natural makeup, it is equally impossible to ignore developmental stages. Diligent mothers may try in futility to train children to do something before they have matured sufficiently. Even if they succeed, they may have damaged the child! Any demand of the child that is inconsistent with his developmental stage may cause psychological damage, which may adversely affect his development and personality, resulting in anxiety, depression and lack of self-confidence. (This applies to even simple things such as hygiene or sitting properly at the table, which mothers often demand prematurely.) (*Alei Shur* vol.1 p. 263).

R' Wolbe suggests that parents learn how to discipline a child in a manner that will result in *an inner desire to do what is right*, rather than out of fear of punishment. He states that parental discipline that is self-centered is counterproductive.

"If a child disobeys, the father feels insulted. He 'punishes' the child for disobeying, but the truth is that this is not 'punishment' but 'vengeance,' which is forbidden by the Torah.

"And what about the parents' desire to gloat over their child's performance? Do they not desire that their friends esteem them because of their child's achievements? If their child disappoints them, they may become angry at the child. Whose benefit are they really seeking, the child's or their own?" (ibid. p.260)

R' Wolbe suggests that physical punishment of a child is less in the interest of correcting a child's behavior than an expression of the parent's anger. This is not healthy discipline.

Several decades ago, there was a movement that preached permissiveness. This was a disaster. It left children totally unprepared to deal with the realities of life. But discipline by coercion is equally ineffective. As Rambam states, the correct path is the median between the two extremes.

Raising children is an awesome responsibility, perhaps the greatest responsibility a person has in one's entire life. It is also undoubtedly the greatest and most challenging task facing a parent. Let us be truthful with ourselves. Would we accept treatment from a doctor or dentist who had as much training in medicine or dentistry as we had in parenting? Would we place our affairs in the hands of an attorney who had as much training in law as we had in parenting? Would we accept treatment or representation from people who had little or no training based on their feeling that they have an intuitive knowledge of their specialty? How can we justify raising our children on our intuition alone?

You may say that you are not raising your children on intuition alone, and that you had adequate training in parenting by observing and remembering how your parents raised you. But are you really pleased with the way you were raised? Perhaps you were one of the fortunate people who did in fact have excellent parenting, but many people have serious complaints about how their parents raised them. They, therefore, did not have good models upon which to base their parenting. If you were not pleased with how your parents raised you, where then did you get training in parenting?

You may say that your displeasure with how you were raised taught you that you must raise your children differently. But that is only a negative statement. Rejection of your parents' method does not yet provide you with a good method.

Perhaps you were so displeased with your parents' ways that you swore, "I'll never do that to my children," and you, therefore, go to the opposite extreme. If your parents were overly strict and controlling, you raise your children with total permissiveness. That, too, is a mistake. Either extreme is unwise. But ironically, studies have shown that people who were raised in a manner that they despised may, in fact, repeat the same pattern with their children.

There is only one reasonable solution. Young people should be trained in proper parenting. Ideally, these issues should be discussed in courses on parenting in the junior and senior years of high school. Consulting a child psychologist when the child has a behavior problem is better than nothing, but it is really too late. It is difficult to undo damage that has resulted from faulty parenting. Inasmuch as there is generally no formal education on parenting in schools, it is crucial that young newlyweds begin to receive training in parenting *before* they have children.

There are instructions and guidelines on discipline. It is not necessary that one adopt everything a certain authority recommends. However, it is important that parents do not take for granted that they are inherently endowed with proper parenting skills. Learning about discipline, thinking about it and discussing it will enable parents to develop parenting skills.

You may say, Why is there a sudden need for training in parenting? We have existed for thousands of years without such training. Why must we have it now?

We have also existed for thousands of years without immunization for whooping cough, diphtheria, lockjaw, measles, mumps and polio. Are you willing to refrain from immunizing your children because your great-grandparents were not immunized?

Furthermore, as mentioned earlier, life in the *shtetl* was nothing like modern living. In previous times, the street was not toxic. Graphic violence and indecency were not piped into the home as it is by television today. There were no electronic games in which the winner was the one who succeeded in killing the most opponents. Pornography was not a billion dollar industry. There were no billboards with explicit immodesty. Youngsters did not come to school with guns. The stresses and temptations to which youngsters are regularly exposed today simply did not exist. Raising a child today is a far more formidable task than ever before.

The following words of R' Wolbe deserve to be placed in every home and displayed with flashing lights. They are the wisest words ever said about parenting: "Parents should learn how to discipline a child in a manner that will result in *an inner desire to do what is right.*" It should be clear that when we say that control is wrong, it does not by any means imply that parents should not discipline a child. Quite the contrary, it means that they should use a method of discipline *that works!*

If we understand that control is illusory, we will be better able to design a method of discipline that is effective and constructive for both parent and child.

Modeling Behavior

There is a general consensus that children learn best by emulating their parents, and that therefore, the most effective way of conveying proper behavior and concepts of right and wrong is *by acting in the ways that we wish our children to act*. Everyone seems to agree that "Do as I say, not as I do," is counterproductive. However, this sometimes seems to be nothing but lip service.

I really do not wish to be abrasive, but I cannot understand how so many people of good intelligence can act so stupidly. In order to prevent children from being exposed to morally corrupt material, the entertainment industry has introduced a system of grading.

Some films are considered, by those who make these decisions appropriate for the entire family, some require parental guidance and some are totally inappropriate for young people. There is no escaping the conclusion that the latter are good only for parents.

A similar grave error was the introduction of a "V-chip," whereby parents can prevent their children from viewing inappropriate programs.

In both cases the message to youngsters is, "These things are good only for daddy and mommy." Anyone with a bit of intelligence would know that these are precisely the things the youngsters will wish to see, and they will manage to see them one way or another. Children want to see what pleases their parents. It is difficult to imagine what could stimulate children more than the knowledge that their parents watch these objectionable films.

No, it is not enough to tell children not to do something. It is not even enough to model our disapproval of improper behavior. Effective modeling depends on *how* it is done.

If you were in a restaurant and found a fly in your bowl of soup, you would call the waiter and have him take it away. If you are extra-sensitive, you may even lose your appetite for the rest of the meal. Insects are disgusting!

What made you feel that way about insects? I'll tell you what. When you were an infant of six months, you saw an ant crossing the blanket or floor. You picked up the insect with your tiny fingers, and did what every baby would do: you tried to put it in your mouth. When your mother saw this, she emitted a cry, shuddered violently, and contorted her face in a way that gave you a clear and intense message that insects are repulsive. That's all you needed to have an abhorrence for insects in your food for the next eighty-nine years.

Suppose mother had not reacted that way, but had said softly, "Honey, please put that little bug down. Bugs are not good to eat." Just how much of an impression would that have made on you?

A sincere emotional expression of disgust can go a long way toward discouraging certain behaviors. If, when any objectionable scenes appeared on the screen, parents would promptly turn off the

TV with a gesture of disgust and horror no less dramatic than when the child puts an insect in his mouth and say, "Yecch! We don't allow trash like that in this house," there would be no need for "V-chips." The child would have an "internal" abhorrence of such scenes.

One of the disciples of R' Mendel of Kotzk related that at one time they were in dire straits, and there was not enough money to buy food. He told the Rebbe that they were expecting a visit from Temerel, a wealthy widow who supported the group, and they would have money. R' Mendl responded, *"Gelt? Feh!"* The disciple said that ever since that time, the sight of money would cause him to feel nauseous.

Actually, this teaching was stated clearly in the Torah thousands of years ago. Strangely enough, we repeat these words several times a day, but do we hear what we are saying?

In the *Shema* we say, "These words *shall be on your heart, and you shall teach them to your children."* Lip service to Torah and mitzvos is not likely to make an impression on children, but if the words of Torah are *on your heart* and you feel them with an intense, heartfelt emotion, then they will carry over to your children.

There was an incident many years ago, where the *mikvah* (ritual bath) in the town was closed for repairs and a man moved out of the town until the *mikvah* was functional. He was not a learned man, just a simple, G–d fearing Jew. His grandchildren are not all fully observant, but they all observe the laws of family purity. Why? Because the importance of this mitzvah had been conveyed to them. It is possible that the grandchildren may not even know about that particular incident, yet its importance was somehow transmitted to them.

The Talmud says that any mitzvah that Jews practiced with great *simchah* has persisted throughout the ages, citing circumcision as example. Again, it is the *emotion* with which a mitzvah is performed that determines its impact on children.

This is true of virtually all behavior. Children are likely to adopt those behaviors that they feel are important to their parents and to avoid those that they feel their parents truly despise.

Parents who wish their children to be Torah observant must be meticulous in observing Torah themselves. It is obvious that parents who violate Shabbos or eat *tereifah* (non-kosher) can hardly expect their children to be Torah observant. But, it should be understood that violation of *any* part of Torah undermines children's devotion to Torah.

Those who are authorities on *mussar* (ethical values) decry the liberties that some people take with those Torah laws that pertain to interpersonal conduct. One may not choose which parts of Torah one wishes to observe. The Talmud says that denying a single letter of the Torah is equivalent to denying *all* of Torah (*Sanhedrin* 99a).

The *halachah* regulating business transactions is every bit as much Torah as the *halachah* prohibiting *tereifah* (forbidden foods). The Talmud says that if a person steals grain, grinds it, bakes it into bread and pronounces the *hamotzi* blessing over it, he is not performing a mitzvah. To the contrary, G–d is angered by the pronunciation of His holy Name over something acquired dishonestly (*Bava Kamma* 94a).

Similarly, *tzedakah* (charity) that is given from money that was acquired dishonestly is not fulfillment of a mitzvah. The authorities point out that the weekly Torah portion instructing donations for the Sanctuary (*Terumah*) is preceded by the portion dealing with the laws of commerce (*Mishpatim*). Only money that is earned in compliance with Torah law may be used for *tzedakah*.

Some people allow themselves to engage in less than totally upright ways of earning money, and they rationalize why they may do so. They should know that they are not fooling G–d, Who is not taken in by their rationalizations. Furthermore, they should know that they are not fooling their children either. Children are exquisitely sensitive and can detect, if only subconsciously, that the parent is compromising Torah law.

When I was in yeshivah in Chicago, I lived with my grandfather. I would visit my home in Milwaukee every few weeks. One time, when I told my grandfather that I was leaving for Milwaukee, he handed me a letter for my father that he was going to mail. He then took out a postage stamp and tore it. "You are not an authorized competitor for the postal service." I learned then how scrupulous one must be in honesty with the government.

Proper *middos* (character traits) are fundamental to Torah observance. When I lecture about improper conduct toward one's spouse, I am often asked, "Can spouse abuse occur among Torah observant people?" My answer is, "Absolutely not! Someone who abuses a spouse is violating *halachah* no less than someone who violates any other *halachah*. Such a person cannot be considered to be Torah observant."

It is not uncommon for children to see a parent express rage. Lecturing to these children about the need to control their anger is not likely to be effective. Hearing a parent tell a "white lie" diminishes a child's respect for truth. Overhearing the parents speaking *lashon hara* (defamatory speech) to each other gives sanction to this transgression. Seeing a parent engage in conversation in shul (synagogue) decreases a child's reverence for G–d.

One might ask, what about a father who is a serious Torah scholar, and his devotion to Torah study is sincere. Why may this father's child deviate from Torah study?

The Talmud was bothered by this question, and offers the insight that often scholars behave condescendingly to unlearned people (*Nedarim* 81a). While these scholars may have accumulated much Torah knowledge, if they are vain and consider themselves superior to others, their Torah knowledge has not refined their characters. Such Torah knowledge is sterile, and may not leave a favorable impression on their children.

The principle I am advocating, *internal* rather than *external* discipline, is hardly novel. This should be the goal of our own behavior, as the Talmud says, "Make His (G–d's) will into your own will, " (*Ethics of the Fathers* 2:4). We are instructed to internalize Torah, so that we do not desire anything other than what Torah teaches. If we truly internalize Torah, our children will sense this and are likely to internalize what we teach them.

Children absorb an attitude toward Torah and Yiddishkeit primarily from their parents. A sincere devotion to the entire Torah, *halachah* and *middos* is the best way to train a child.

The Key to Internalization

For a child to internalize the parent's will, three conditions must be met; (1) the child must love the parent, (2) the child must respect the parent and (3) the child must know that the parent's instructions are in the interest of the child rather than the parent.

Let us begin with the last item. "Make His will your will," internalization of G–d's will, is dependent on our awareness that the mitzvos were given for *our* betterment and not to provide for G–d's pleasure. This is clearly stated in the Midrash. "What difference could it make to G–d whether an animal is ritually slaughtered or is put to death in some other manner? The mitzvos were given to refine people's character" (*Tanchuma, Shemini* 7:8). We must understand that if we sin, we are harming ourselves, not G–d. G–d is all-perfect, and He is not enriched by our mitzvos nor impoverished by our sins. "If you have sinned, what change have you made in Him, and if you have many transgressions, what have you done to Him? If you are righteous, what have you given Him, or what does He take from you?" (*Job* 35:6-7).

If a person thinks he is doing G–d a favor by observing Torah, it is understandable that if he is displeased by what happens to him or by the injustices one sees in the world, he may act out by deviating from Torah or by doing things to spite G–d. If a person knows that observance of the mitzvos is for *his own* welfare, then it would be foolish to harm himself because he may be angry at G–d.

For children to internalize parental will, they must *feel* that it is primarily – if not solely – for their betterment. This is a key condition, and it is not easy to achieve. Parents may believe that they are acting only in the children's interest, but this is not always completely so. Let me cite an extreme example.

Parents consulted me in desperation. Their daughter had revealed to them that she had fallen in love with a non-Jewish man and they were planning to be married. Understandably, the parents were devastated by this, and I empathized with them, feeling their pain. But some of the things they said indicated that their concern was not totally for their daughter's welfare. The mother said, "How could she do this to us, after all we have done for her?" I believe that intermarriage is a serious mistake and a source of eventual distress for the couple. A more appropriate statement would have been, "What is she doing to *herself*? Is there any way she can be helped to see that this is self-destructive?" This would be more effective than, "What is she doing to us?"

Among other things, the father said, "How will I be able to face my friends or show myself in shul?" I am certain that the daughter sensed this attitude. Blinded by passion, she might nevertheless have had a second thought if she were helped to feel that she was harming herself. As much as she cared for her parents, her father's fear of being embarrassed was not enough to overcome her passion.

Some youngsters who attended after-school-hours Hebrew school were very verbal in expressing their displeasure. Their friends were playing football while they were sitting in a classroom, learning very little of substance. They felt that their four-year ordeal in Hebrew school was for the sole purpose of their having a Bar Mitzvah so that their parents could throw a lavish party to impress their friends. The children knew that the Hebrew school education was for little else. Becoming Bar Mitzvah was not so that he should put on *tefillin* (phylacteries), because his father never does. It was not to become a "son of mitzvos," which is what "Bar Mitzvah" means. The parents did not keep kosher nor observe Shabbos. Sitting in Hebrew class for four years and being deprived of sharing in their friends' fun just so the parents could have a ritual service and a party was not fair.

I do not doubt that most parents sincerely love their children, but that is not enough. We love our eyes, ears and hands. We protect them from injury because they are part of us. Our children are also part of us. We rejoice in their happiness and suffer in their distress. True. But for children to internalize the parents' will, they must feel that the parents' love goes beyond their being an extension of the parents.

When I see two- and three-year-old children wearing expensive designer clothes, I cannot but think, were these really bought for the child's benefit because they are of better quality, or was it perhaps because the parents want others to see that their child wears designer clothes?

Children did not ask to be brought into a world fraught with stresses and challenges. If they feel that they were conceived because the parents truly wished to fulfill the mitzvah of having children, their attitude towards fulfilling the parents' will is more positive. If they feel that they are here primarily to provide for the parents' emotional needs, they may not feel too kindly about tolerating the difficulties in life. One patient angrily exclaimed, "I'm sick and tired of being a *nachas* (pleasure to parents) machine."

If we want our children to have an internalized discipline, we should enable them to truly feel that it is for their welfare rather than ours.

The Torah obligates us to respect and revere our parents (*Exodus* 20:12, *Leviticus* 19:3). Fulfillment of this mitzvah is greatly facilitated when parents have earned respect and reverence. Parents who have not acted in a way that merits respect and reverence will find that their children can hardly internalize their will.

Finally, internalization requires that children love their parents. The Torah requires that we accord parents respect and reverence. These behaviors can be commanded. Love is an emotion that cannot be legislated.

Solomon says, "As water reflects face to face, so the heart of person to person" (*Proverbs* 27:19). True love is reciprocal.

Let us remember that part of parents' love for children is essentially a variety of self-love because our children are extensions of ourselves. This particular kind of love cannot be reciprocated because parents are *not* extensions of their children. The love that *can* be reciprocated is an unconditional love that is beyond the self-love. If parents feel it and demonstrate it, the children are likely to reciprocate.

There are, of course, a variety of ways whereby parents can show their love for their children. Physical contact is just one of them, but it is an important one. A classic study on infants showed that babies who were cared for in a foundling home and had no cuddling during the first six months of life developed serious emotional problems. Even later in life, physical demonstration of affection is important.

Some parents may have difficulty embracing or kissing their children. This may be due to factors in their own development. If they are aware of this, they would be wise to receive therapy to overcome this inhibition.

A young man came to Pittsburgh for treatment of a severe alcoholism problem. He had been abusive in his marriage, which had been terminated. He made good progress in treatment.

One morning it occurred to me that this was the day this young man was to be discharged from treatment, and I wished to say goodbye to him. I called the facility, and was told that he had just left for the airport. Inasmuch as I pass the airport on the way to the treatment center, I stopped off and found that he had boarded the plane. This was prior to the days of maximum security precautions, and since I was well known at the airport, they allowed me to board the plane for a few moments.

The young man was surprised to see me. I embraced him, wished him good luck and kissed him. His eyes grew misty, and in a broken voice he said, "That is the first time in my life anyone has ever kissed me." How tragic that a person of thirty-one cannot recall ever receiving a kiss from a parent!

I cannot restrain myself from sharing some personal data. When my children were tots, my parents would visit, and my father would get down on the floor to play with them. He embraced and kissed them. My mother's eyes welled up with tears. "It makes me so happy to see that. In our home, show of affection was so restricted. I was not permitted to kiss my father, except occasionally on his hand."

My grandfather was Rabbi Benzion Halberstam, the Bobover Rebbe, a great *tzaddik*. I do not question *tzaddikim*. I am certain he had valid reasons for his ways. My mother had enormous reverence for her great father, and I am sure that she loved him. But her tears indicated that she would have been far happier had he been more demonstrative.

Perhaps there was a misconception that showing affection to children could detract from the reverence they should have. My uncle, the late Rabbi Shlomo Halberstam, the previous Bobover Rebbe, showed great affection to his children and grandchildren. Not only did they love him deeply, but their reverence for him was not diminished in the least.

Not only was my father demonstrative of his love for us, but we also felt intensely how much he cared for us. If one of my children was sick, I would wake up at 6 AM to find my father peering through the front door window. He was anxious to know how the child felt, but waited until he saw some movement in the house. He would not knock on the door and risk waking us up.

I never recall my father punishing me nor shouting at me. I was hardly a saint as a child, and if I did something that warranted a reprimand, he would say softly, *Es past nisht* (that is not becoming of you). I was not made to feel bad for what I had done. To the contrary, I was told I was too good, and that whatever I had done was beneath my dignity. At the risk of being accused of boasting, I believe that I did internalize my parents' will. They made it easy for me to do so.

Although I have written this elsewhere, I repeat it here because it demonstrates how effective discipline can be practiced without causing a child to feel that he is bad.

When I was nine and ten, I was a chess prodigy. Many of the worshippers in my father's shul were Russian immigrants who earned their livelihood as peddlers. They would come to shul early for *minchah* (afternoon service) and play chess while drinking scalding hot tea. I watched them play chess, learned the game and soon beat these seasoned players.

One Rosh Hashanah afternoon, a rabbi from Chicago who was our guest for the holiday asked me if I wished to play chess. "But it's *yom tov,*" I said. The rabbi assured me that playing chess on *yom tov* was permissible. I beat him twice.

On the second night of Rosh Hashanah, the *shammes* (beadle) told me, "The rabbi wants to see you in the study." My father was looking into a *sefer* (Torah volume), and I waited respectfully to be acknowledged. After a few moments he looked up and said, "You played chess on Rosh Hashanah?" I said, "Yes. Rabbi C. said it was permissible."

My father did not say a word. He returned to his *sefer* and shook his head barely perceptibly, but enough to convey his disapproval. The message was that while playing chess on *yom tov* may be technically permissible, it was inappropriate. Rosh Hashanah is a solemn day, and playing games may detract from its solemn character.

I accepted the reprimand, and waited to be dismissed by *"Geh gezunderheit"* (Go in good health). My father let me stand there a few minutes to make sure I had absorbed the reprimand. Then he looked up and with a twinkle in his eye he said, "Did you checkmate him?" "Twice," I said. He nodded, *"Geh gezunderheit."*

My father had never read a book on parenting, but his skill was intuitive. He had delivered the necessary reprimand, but he would not allow me to leave the room with a negative feeling. He was proud that I had defeated the rabbi twice.

My father's reprimand was teaching rather than controlling. I look back upon that incident with fondness. Control does not produce cherished memories. Teaching does.

What *Is* the Parent's Will?

f we want our children to internalize our will, it is only sensible to let them know just what that will is. This may seem to be a subtle and even trivial point, but it is nevertheless important. *Let us try to minimize our instructions of what we want them to do, and phrase our instructions more in terms of our will.*

Let me explain by using an example from my work with alcoholics. A woman called, complaining about her husband's heavy drinking. He is an executive who functions efficiently at the office. However, he is impossible to live with. When he drinks, he becomes abusive. He thinks of no one but himself, and he terrorizes the children. She has pleaded with him to get help so that he can stop drinking, but he denies that there is anything wrong. He blames everything on her. "What can I do to get him to stop drinking?"

I gently tried to explain to the woman that as long as her husband does not think that he has a drinking problem, there is nothing she can do make him change. I suggested that inasmuch as his drinking is causing her great distress, she should see a therapist with expertise in helping family members of alcoholics, and that she should join a family support group.

"But what can I do about his drinking problem?" she asked.

I said, "My dear woman, your husband does not have a drinking problem. *You* have the drinking *problem*. Your husband has the drinking *solution*."

This was not just a witticism. The person who has the headache is the one who has the problem and seeks relief. As long as the drinking was not causing her husband any discomfort, he was not going to seek help. *She* was the one who was suffering. Therefore, she should seek help for herself.

The purpose of this story is to focus on just who it is that has a problem. When a child behaves in a way that annoys the parents, who has the problem, the child or the parent? Invariably, it is the parent. It might help if this is made clear.

For example, the kids have left their jackets strewn around the house. Mother may say, "How many times have I told you to hang up your things when you come in? Now get those jackets in the closet where they belong." Obviously, the kids have no problem with the jackets being wherever they are. It is the mother for whom it is a problem, so why not say so? "I don't like clothes lying all over the house. I try to keep the house neat and clean." No orders. Just a true statement that she is unhappy with things the way the are.

It is possible that the kids won't budge. However, they are more likely to hang up their jackets than if she had ordered them to do so.

Dr. Thomas Gordon elaborates on this in his book, *Discipline That Works*. He refers to the superiority of "I" messages over "You" messages. While there is no guarantee that "I" messages will always be effective, Dr. Gordon cites studies that indicate that they are more effective than "You" messages.

Dr. Gordon states that children react defensively to "You" messages. They feel that "You" messages are a put-down. For example, "You are driving me crazy," or "You ought to know better than that," are clearly put-downs. Children resent this and may want to "get back" at whoever put them down. On the other hand, "I" messages contain a less negative evaluation of the child and do not injure the relationship. He cites a teacher who reported that when she told the children, "When you mix the paints and spill them all over the sink and table, I have to scrub up later or get yelled at by the custodian. I'm sick of cleaning up after you, and I feel helpless to prevent it from happening," she got much better results than when she would order them to clean up.

Dr. Gordon points out that when children are given "I" messages, they have to come up with a solution to the problem, and that children actually take pride in this. That cannot happen with "You" messages. He emphasizes, *"We tend to underestimate kids' capacity to change until they're given a chance to show it."*

I tend to agree with Dr. Gordon. As I said, I don't recall my father ever spanking me or shouting at me. One phrase is indelibly etched in my mind. When I was eleven years old, I did something that I am not proud of. My father sat me down and said, "Until you become Bar Mitzvah, I am responsible for your sins. It never dawned upon me that when the Torah prohibited what you did, it had me in mind." Not only did I keenly feel his pain, but sixty-one years later that phrase still reverberates in my mind. I have long since overcome the guilt engendered by what I did. I have not carried that baggage for sixty-one years. I did not resent my father for his rebuke. Perhaps it was because I felt that I should do something to make up for the pain I caused him that I was subsequently able to bring him a great deal of *nachas*. My love for him grew. I don't know what my reaction would have been had he delivered a scathing "You" message which I richly deserved.

As I think back upon that event, I realize how bad I felt that my father was hurting because of something that I did. If I had not loved him, that would not have been a deterrent. My reaction was a result of my love and respect for him, and my love and respect for him increased as a result of the way he handled my misbehavior.

The Talmud states that the high priest, Aaron, "loved people and brought them closer to Torah" (*Ethics of the Fathers* 1:12). If Aaron knew that a person had committed a sin, he would go out of his way to befriend him. The next time the person was tempted to sin, he thought, "How will I be able to face Aaron if I do this?" Was this not a reprimand? Yes, a powerful reprimand of love. A sharp rebuke might have resulted in the person rationalizing his actions or becoming defensively defiant.

A man complained to the Baal Shem Tov that his son was going "off the *derech*" (deviating from the path of Torah). The Baal Shem Tov said, "Show him extra love. He needs it most."

Showing extra love should not be done in a way that would appear to be rewarding improper behavior. Children must be taught what is wrong and that improper behavior will not be tolerated. However, when the opportunity for showing love occurs, it should not be overlooked.

There are times, albeit rare, when a judicious spanking may be justifiable. If a small child runs into the road to retrieve his ball, he may not be able to understand the explanation that oncoming traffic can be very dangerous. At such an occasion, an angry sounding "No! No! No! You don't run into the street after the ball!" accompanied by a single mild *potsch* (slap) on the part of the anatomy designed for it is appropriate. But this is effective only *immediately* after the act. A spanking given later is of no value.

But even a spanking can be delivered in a non-injurious but very effective way. When my younger brother was about four, he went out the upstairs window and sat on the slanted roof beneath. My father softly called him in, realizing that shouting might alarm him and cause him to fall. When he came in, my father said in a definite "no nonsense" tone of voice, "You don't ever go out on the roof again." He held my brother's hand in his, and delivered a sharp blow *to his own hand*. The child was not injured in the least, and the message was conveyed emphatically.

A student in the yeshivah of my uncle, the late Bobover Rebbe, played "hookey" from class. The Rebbe called him in, and firmly told him that for what he did, he deserved a *potsch*. He then softly caressed his cheek and said, "Let this be the equivalent of a *potsch.*" The student never skipped class again, and decades later, fondly recalls that *potsch*.

It is not the pain of the *potsch* that is the deterrent. Rather, it is the clear demonstration of disapproval. It may well be that my father's painless *potsch* was even more effective because the child did not have to deal with the pain, only with the disapproval. Pain might have actually negated the intensity and the effectiveness of the disapproval, because the child may have reacted defensively to the pain.

The "I" message technique does not stand in isolation, and unrealistic expectations will result in disappointment. It is part of Dr. Gordon's system of discipline, which requires parental training. His book, *Discipline that Works,* is worthwhile reading.

There are authorities on child rearing who feel that an authoritarian approach can be most effective, and each expert can cite studies for their claims and counterclaims. It may well be that each method is effective *if practiced with consistency*. Furthermore, some experts on childrearing have parent groups that meet regularly to exchange ideas and information. Participating in such groups may enhance *any* modality of childrearing.

Minimizing Resistance

Once we accept the fact that absolute control is both impossible and ineffective, we can look for more effective ways to achieve compliance with parental wishes, and encourage internalization of behavioral controls. This means that children are helped to learn and develop internal controls.

The human tendency to desire what is prohibited is literally as old as the world itself. Adam and Eve had everything a person could possibly want. They were literally in *Gan Eden* (Paradise). There was only one tree whose fruit was forbidden, and that was the one whose fruit they ate.

We may safely assume that it is inherent in people to resist orders. If they comply, it may be because they feel compelled to do so, but as we have said, they may not internalize the rules.

There are some things that are not negotiable. In a Torah observant family, there can be no compromise on how much of Shabbos one may keep. Everyone is equally bound by *halachah,* and except where one's health is endangered, there are no dispensations. No one, no parent, no rabbi, no group of rabbis, have the authority to override *halachah.* It is precisely this universal deference to *halachah* that everyone can model for children.

There is a companion statement in Talmud to "Make His will your will," and that is, "Set aside your will before His" (*Ethics of the Fathers* 2:4). This is a statement of deference to authority.

We model deference to authority when we refrain from doing something that we would really like to do because an authority has instructed us so. This is not as simple as it sounds. The Talmud says that a person should not say, "I detest pork," but rather, "I might like pork, but G–d has forbidden it" (*Rashi, Leviticus* 20:26). Most observant people have developed such an antipathy to pork that they could never say, "I might like pork, but G–d has forbidden it." For many observant families, desisting from what Torah has forbidden has become second nature. We may have to search for things that we might like and that we avoid *only* because a Torah authority has ruled that it is forbidden.

One area where we can model deference to authority is in avoidance of *lashon hara* (defamatory speech). Quite frequently, conversation within the family turns to talking about what someone said or did that was not praiseworthy. At this point, a parent should say, "I'm really curious to know what happened, but my curiosity will have to go unsatisfied. Talking this way is *lashon hara,* which the Torah forbids." This is a clear statement that the parent is willing to forego fulfilling a desire in deference to *halachah,* and it is a powerful modeling. Other things may be found which are not as reprehensible to us as pork, and of which we can say, "I'd really like to do that, but it is not permissible."

Western civilization, especially the United States, worships at the shrine of democracy. Democracy in government may seem the most fair, but G–d's world is not a democracy. No popular referendum can change one word of Torah. The authority of G–d cannot be challenged.

It is obvious that the family cannot operate as a democracy. If it did, then the kids would vote that all meals should consist of hot dogs with mustard, or ice cream and popcorn. School would be voted out, and the kids could run around at night until they fell asleep on the living room floor. Clearly the parents must wield authority. A family must operate and abide by rules.

Even if it were conceded that wielding absolute authority is best in principle, the fact is that it is generally not feasible. It is evident that exerting absolute authority, at least in modern times, is not likely to be successful, and that children imbued with the noble ideas of "human rights" will simply not yield to absolute authority. Rules must be enforced, but we must find a practical way of implementing rules.

One way is that in establishing household rules of a non-*halachic* nature, we should look for opportunities where the children can participate in drawing up the rules. For example, mother may say, "I prepare the supper meals, but you should clear the table and stack the dishwasher. How would you like to schedule that?" The children may decide that Shmuel will take Sundays and Tuesdays, and Rifki will take Mondays and Wednesdays. Because Friday night dishes are done together with Shabbos dishes on Shabbos night, they can trade off Thursdays and Shabbos. Whichever, the children can work out their own schedule, and may trade days if they wish.

Having children participate in establishing household rules enhances their motivation to adhere to them. The final act that sparked the American revolution was the "Stamp Act," which gave rise to the slogan, "No taxation without representation." It is simply common sense that having a voice in being taxed lessens the resistance to compliance. It also elevates the children's self-esteem to know that their opinion is considered valuable. In one of my books I quoted a psychologist who said, "If you have given your children self-esteem, you have given them everything. If you have not given them self-esteem, whatever else you have given them is of little value." I am not certain that parents can "give" their children self-esteem, but we certainly should avail ourselves of every opportunity to contribute to it. Enlisting children in decision-making is one such opportunity.

While it may be true that "Father knows best," it is only logical that "Father plus children know even better." Let us not underestimate children's ingenuity. They may come up with ideas that did not occur to us.

The Talmud says, "Fortunate is the generation where the greater are willing to listen to the lesser" (*Rosh Hashanah* 25b). Let me share an example.

When I was on the staff of a state mental hospital, we would have a group of medical students visit every few weeks. This gave them the opportunity to see rare cases of mental illnesses that they had read about in textbooks. I conducted one such tour, and pointed out to the students the most senior patient in the hospital. He had been admitted fifty years earlier, and he had not spoken a single word during those fifty years. During all his waking hours, he would stand in the corner of the ward, assuming a grotesque position. All medications, treatments and attempts at persuasion had not been successful in getting him to sit on a bench for even a few minutes.

One of the medical students asked for permission to talk to this patient. He said to him, "Why don't you sit down and rest a bit?" The patient gave him a blank stare. The student said, "Look. You can sit down, and I'll do this for you." He then assumed the grotesque posture of the patient, and the patient promptly sat down on the bench for the first time in fifty years!

What can we make of this? Perhaps the patient's deluded mind made him think that by assuming the peculiar posture, he was holding up the world. He was able to relinquish this awesome responsibility only if it were assumed by someone else. Whether or not this is the explanation, the fact is that a young medical student had found a solution to a problem that had defied the skills of countless psychiatrists!

It is related that the Baal Shem Tov once stood in prayer for an extended period of time. His disciples gradually left, and he then concluded his praying. He said to them, "When a person wishes to reach something high, he may stand on someone's shoulders. If the supporting person leaves, he comes down to the ground. As long as you were with me, I stood on your shoulders and could reach celestial heights. When you left, I was unable to do so."

As wise as parents may be, they may actually increase their wisdom by listening to their children's opinions. Obviously, many juvenile ideas are inappropriate, but you may be pleasantly surprised at children's ingenuity. Furthermore, even if their ideas are rejected, the fact that you listened to them contributes to self-discipline and to self-esteem.

It is also advisable to make reasonable compromises. One night, everybody leaves the table, and mother says, "Hey! Whose turn is it to clear the table tonight?" Shmuel says, "It is Rifki's."

Rifki says, "I have to be on the phone with Esther for about an hour to get the stuff I need for a paper I have to hand in tomorrow. Can't you do it tonight, Shmuly?"

"Heck, no," Shmuly says. "I'm going to hockey practice."

Rifki says, "I'll do it as soon as I get off the phone with Esther. O.K.?"

"O.K.," mother says.

The job gets done, and the children feel they participated in the decision and were not "bossed around."

Participation and compromise, where reasonable, may take off the sharp bite of being ordered to do something.

Some parents may say, "No way! In my father's home there was no participation and no compromise. Rules were obeyed, or else!" In your father's home there may not have been air-conditioning or a microwave. In many ways, our circumstances differ from our parents'. As long as we do not compromise on *halachah,* reasonable flexibility is expedient.

Children are much more likely to comply with parents' wishes if they feel that the parents understand their needs. They can accept a refusal of a request much better when it is not dogmatic. "Because I said so" is likely to elicit resistance.

Some requests may be unreasonable and must be refused. Children may not accept the explanation for the refusal. Even adults may be impervious to logical explanations when they have a strong desire for something. But even if children do not accept an explanation, their attitude is likely to be less oppositional if they are aware that the parents at least understand their needs. Children should be encouraged to state their needs and explain what they want. Adults' perspective of things and children's perspective may be very divergent. We should try to understand how children see things, and that is not a simple task. However, if parents can *truthfully* say, "I understand," the child will feel this and will be much more apt to be cooperative than if he feels that the parents are not taking his needs into consideration.

If the child is compelled to do something he does not want to do, the parent wins. If the parent doesn't want to make a fuss and gives in to the child, the child wins. *Whenever one wins, the other loses.* Losing does not make for happiness. A loser generally feels some anger toward the victor. We can increase happiness in the family by trying to avoid anyone's losing.

Control by Guilt or Pity

Guilt is a powerful weapon which can cause severe and enduring injury. Unfortunately its use to wield control is widespread.

"You are going to be the death of me yet." "You are giving your father a heart attack." "Look what you have done to the family." These and other expressions are used in the attempt to make others do or not do something.

In addition to being injurious, control by guilt detracts from the issue itself. Instead of trying to understand what is motivating the person's behavior and trying to address the person's needs that has led him to the behavior of which one disapproves, the controlling attempt is to deter the person from doing what he feels he needs by invoking threats. This generally does not work. If a person is driven to do something by a need, he is unlikely to desist because of threats. He will go ahead with what he wishes to do, and in addition, will bear resentment for being threatened.

I work with people addicted to alcohol and drugs. To the best of my knowledge, no alcoholic has stopped drinking because his wife has said, "Look what you are doing to the children." If anything, the alcoholic will drink even more to kill the pain of the guilt. No youngster has quit using drugs because, "You're giving your father a heart attack." Understanding what is driving the youngster to use drugs may not stop him, but it can lead the way to a constructive approach. Instead of threatening, the parents may go for counseling, which is more likely to result in getting the youngster to accept treatment. Guilt does not accomplish this.

Once the seed of guilt is planted, it is most difficult to uproot. A thirty-four-year-old woman went into a deep depression after her father, an overweight smoker, died of a heart attack. As a teenager, she had acted out, and her mother told her, "You're killing your father." Twenty years later, when his smoking and obesity resulted in a heart attack, she was haunted by the feeling that she was responsible for her father's death.

Guilt can serve a purpose when it makes a person feel bad for what he did and motivates him to do *teshuvah* (repentance, atonement). We can see the Torah's attitude toward guilt from the prophet's statement, "I have erased your iniquities like a fog and your sins like a cloud" (*Isaiah* 44:22). "And all the sins of Your nation, the House of Israel, cast away to a place where they will neither be remembered, considered nor brought to mind— ever" (*Micah* 7:19). Guilt should not endure. If a person has in fact done wrong, he should do whatever is necessary for *teshuvah* and then be free of guilt. This does not happen when guilt is used for control.

We make mistakes, and we are indeed responsible for our actions. We should make amends and restitution whenever possible. However, no one should be condemned and given a life-sentence of suffering for a mistake.

Just as parents may try to control their children by guilt, children may do the same to parents. Some misguided psychologists think they are helping their patients when they blame parents for their emotional problems. Firstly, most parents do the best they know how, and even if they did not employ the best parenting skills, they should not be condemned for their good intentions. Secondly, even if parents were derelict, blaming them is not going to make the patient's life better. When my patients blame their parents, I say to them, "Even if you are today what your parents made you, it is your job to change yourself. If you stay this way, it is your fault, not your parents'."

Every so often I hear on the media that Jews are still trying to control the world by the guilt of the Holocaust. It is not the guilt to which we refer, but to the distrust that we have of a world that condoned it. We know that hundreds of thousands of Jews could have been saved had the United States bombed the railroad tracks leading to the death camps. There is documented evidence of this. We distrust a world that gave asylum to inhuman fiends like Mengele. We distrust a church which launched the Inquisition, which gave its blessing to the massacres of the Crusades and which was silent during the Holocaust.

Akin to control by guilt is control by illness. I know this personally because, I am ashamed to admit, I used it.

When I was ten, our family doctor gave me a medication for hayfever which knocked me out. On examination, the doctor told my father that I had a heart murmur. My father had a fanatic concern about his children's health, and I played the heart murmur for all it was worth. I managed to stay out of school for four months!

We should do all we can to help a sick person. That is the great mitzvah of *bikur cholim* (visiting and helping the sick). But we should not be *controlled* by someone's illness, and we should not exploit illness to control others.

I knew a man who was an obnoxious person. He suffered a severe heart attack, and because his health was precarious, people were afraid to confront him. One person said, "If Jack ever fully recovers, there will be a line a block long of people waiting to punch him in the face." People tolerated his behavior, but it made him no friends.

The ultimate fallacy in control is the threat of suicide. It is flawed both on the part of the controller and the controlee. Giving in to a suicidal threat is like paying blackmail: There is no end to it. If it works, it may be used again and again.

A husband who refuses to accept the reality that the marriage is over may say, "If you leave me, I'll kill myself," and may underscore this by taking a less-than-lethal overdose. If the wife is frightened by this threat, she has given him a weapon that he can use repeatedly to discourage the separation or for any other purpose.

A woman was drinking excessively and using drugs. Her husband, mother and grown children all confronted her, saying, "Unless you go for treatment, we are simply not going to have anything to do with you." She responded, "If you walk out on me, I'll kill myself." She continued drinking and using drugs and they did not execute their threat. She has continued making her family miserable with her addiction, and of course, is slowly killing herself.

When there is a risk of suicide due to depression, a psychiatrist should be consulted immediately for guidance. Suicide is most horrific and one should *not* rely on the misinformation that "those who threaten don't do it." If a psychiatrist determines that the person has a depressive disorder, then the necessary treatment should be implemented. If a psychiatrist determines that the suicide threat is manipulative, the response should be something like, "Look my dear (husband, wife, son, daughter, etc.), if you carry out your threat to kill yourself, I will feel very sad, because I care for you a great deal. However, I will *not* feel guilty. I will seek the best possible advice and guidance on how to handle our circumstances, and I will do what is determined to be the right and proper thing, which will be in your best interest as well as mine." One must indeed obtain expert counseling on the particular situation, but one cannot allow manipulation and control by suicidal threats.

What happens if the person, G–d forbid, does carry out the threat? If competent counseling and thorough consideration resulted in the steps one took, then one should not feel guilty for doing what was right. There is simply no way one can yield to such blackmail.

Closely related to control by guilt is control by pity. You may feel so sorry for someone that you give in to his wishes.

Hannah was a bright young woman who was a social worker. One of her clients was a young man, an immigrant who had no family. Hannah's mothering instinct overtook her and she desperately wanted to help him. She did not safeguard her professional boundaries, and when he told her that he had nothing to eat, she told him he could come to her house for dinner. This occurred several times, and she also lent him a few dollars here and there. Eventually they began dating in what was a very unhealthy relationship.

Hannah realized that this relationship was bad, and she told Steven that she could no longer see him. He preyed on her sympathies, and she agreed to see him again. This on-again off-again relationship lasted for two years. Steven could get only unskilled labor jobs. In spite of her better judgment and against the advice of her parents, Hannah married Steven.

Soon after the marriage, Hannah realized she had made a serious mistake. She did not have the courage to tell Steven that she wanted out. Steven was aware, even if only subconsciously, that he could control Hannah because of her pity for him. Soon he did not even look for work, but stayed in the house and watched television while Hannah supported them. Perhaps because he felt this was demeaning for him, he began berating her, constantly criticizing everything she did.

Hannah felt trapped, and began to drink in order to escape her misery. Eventually her drinking escalated, resulting in her being hospitalized for alcoholism. Now Steven really had the upper hand, being the long-suffering husband of an alcoholic wife.

During the treatment for alcoholism, Hannah overcame her denial of the sick relationship, and realized how wrong it was to let herself be controlled by her pity for Steven. She suggested that

Steven get into therapy to overcome his pathologic dependency, but Steven would not hear of it. Eventually the marriage was terminated, but Hannah had suffered deeply for years.

Whether by authority, guilt, threats, illness, pity or any other way, control never makes friends. Control by passive dependency is not uncommon. Let us look at this a bit more closely.

Passive Control

ontrol does not always come in the form of exercising authority or overt domination. A very common control technique, which is often not recognized as such, is *control by passivity*. This may be subdivided into two categories: passive-dependent and passive-aggressive.

An infant is an example of normal passive-dependency. The infant is truly helpless. It cannot get food by itself or take care of any other needs. When the infant cries or gives any other indication of being in need, the parents respond. The infant who cries at night makes the parent get out of bed to see what is wrong and remedy it. The parents realize that they have the responsibility of caring for the infant, and they respond to its expression of its needs. You might say that the infant *controls* the parents by its helplessness and dependence on them. However, this is a healthy control.

The picture changes drastically when the dependent subject is not an infant, but a full-grown adult who presents himself as helpless. Here are some of the manifestations of a passive-dependent adult. Not all of them need be present.

- He is unable to make everyday decisions, and allows others to make important decisions for him, e.g., where to live or what job to take.
- He agrees with people even when he thinks they are wrong, because he fears being rejected if he disagrees.
- He has difficulty initiating or doing things on his own.
- He volunteers to do things that are unpleasant in order to get people to like him (people-pleasing).
- He feels uncomfortable or helpless when alone.
- He feels devastated when close relationships end.
- He is frequently preoccupied with fears of being abandoned.
- He is easily and deeply hurt by criticism or disapproval.

Let us look a bit closer at some of these behaviors.

The difficulty in making important decisions is due to a lack of self-confidence and trust in one's own judgment. A person is afraid that he may make the wrong decision and does not want the responsibility for this. When decisions must be made and he avoids doing so, he essentially *forces* others to make the decision. By forcing others to do so, he exerts a kind of control over them. Similarly, by avoiding initiating or doing things on his own, he makes others initiate or do them. And, of course, if things do not turn out well, he can put the blame on others.

Some of these features may be rather harmless. For example, when a child can dress himself, it is normal for a mother to put out his clothes for him. When a husband has no idea of what he should wear, and the wife has to put out his clothes for him every day, that may be passive dependence. If in every other aspect of life the husband is assertive and functional, this dependency on his wife is no big deal. It is possible that he has no concept of color combinations, and may wear a bizarre combination of suit, tie and socks. If he is truly helpless, then his dependence is not pathologic. If he is so rushed for time that preparing his clothes for him is expedient, that, too, is not pathologic. However, if he is capable of doing it and places the chore on his wife, that is passive-dependence.

One might think that volunteering to do things for others is always a noble mitzvah of *chesed* (kindness). It is indeed so when the person does it because it is a mitzvah, the right and proper thing to do, because then he is truly doing it for someone else. When one does *chesed*, one has a good feeling. If he does so because he wants to ingratiate himself with others, he is doing it primarily *for himself* rather than for them. People who are "people-pleasers" generally do not feel good about what they do for others. They feel compelled to do it for fear of rejection, and they often resent what they are doing.

Small children may not want their parents to leave them with a baby-sitter. Of course, they should be made to feel safe with a responsible baby-sitter. Their discomfort when their parents leave is understandable, and they should eventually grow out of this dependency. An otherwise healthy adult who is uncomfortable or fears being alone and clings to others suffers a pathologic dependence.

Feeling grief when a valued relationship ends is normal and healthy. Appropriate mourning and working through one's grief allow the person to resume normal life activities and cope with the reality of a loss. A passive-dependent person may not be able to do so. He may exploit his loss not only to gain sympathy but to get others to do things for him, claiming that he is too crushed to be able to function normally.

There are halachic guidelines for *chesed*. If a person is unable to do something and you help him do it, that is *chesed*. If he *can* do it himself but wants you to do it for him, that is not *chesed*. This can be seen by the mitzvah of helping a person take the load off his beast of burden. The Torah says "assist him in doing it" (*Exodus* 23:5), which means that he does his share and you help him. If, however, he sits idly by and says, "You have the mitzvah, so you do it," then it is not a mitzvah.

Doing things for others that they can do for themselves, unless there is a legitimate reason, encourages them to be dependent. They may fail to develop their skills and a sense of responsibility. If they are in fact capable of something but *think* they are helpless, doing it for them *reinforces their feelings of helplessness*. It is obvious that making a person pathologically dependent cannot be a mitzvah.

Sometimes our motivation is not "people-pleasing" but a feeling of pity. A person may tell you a tale of woe and you feel so sorry for him that you want to do something for him. If he has indeed suffered and you can do something which will relieve his suffering in a way that is constructive for him, that is a great mitzvah. *If he controls you by making you feel sorry for him*, that is not healthy. That is yielding to control and reinforcing the other person's need and way of controlling.

Sometimes, refusing to help may appear cruel, but it may be the right thing to do. A person who has suffered a disability of an arm or leg may have difficulty walking or doing things. The rehabilitation specialist may give precise instructions as to how much you may help him, because forcing him to make the extra effort to do things for himself, even though it may be difficult for him, may be necessary for regaining the strength of the limb. In such situations, it is understandable that one feels sorry for the person, but if one does not follow the instructions of the specialist, one is actually hindering the recovery.

A person who is so sensitive that he responds to constructive criticism by moping or crying may discourage others from correcting him. If you are afraid to correct him because you do not wish to precipitate his reaction, you are allowing him *to control you*. It is appropriate to give truly constructive criticism so that a person does not repeat his mistakes. If you are reluctant to do so because he may feel bad, you are allowing him to control you and keep you from doing what is right.

Reinforcing pathologic dependency lowers a person's self-esteem. Doing this is hardly a kindness.

There is a second variety of passivity, *passive-aggressive*, which is used as control. Passive-aggressive behavior can be most frustrating, if not maddening.

Aggression may be difficult to deal with, but at least it is open and above board. When the aggression is concealed under a cloak of passivity, it can be disarming.

I am reminded of a patient whom I treated during my residency training. She was hospitalized for depression. Many depressions are due to a biochemical imbalance and are often treatable with appropriate medications to correct the imbalance. Grandma Frances' (that's what everyone called her) depression was not due to a chemical imbalance and it did not respond to medication. Grandma Frances *used* her depression to control people. Grandma Frances was passive-aggressive rather than depressed. She was negativistic. Here is an example of how she controlled people.

Grandma Frances initiated an activity — making cloth dolls for the children in Children's Hospital. She taught the other women how to do it, and made them feel guilty if they did not do enough to help the poor sick children. One evening the patients were told that there was a movie in the auditorium. All the women got up to go to the movie, except Grandma Frances. The women said, "Grandma, aren't you coming with us to the movie?" Grandma answered, "No, you can go to the movie and enjoy yourself. I'm going to stay here and make dolls for the poor sick children in Children's Hospital." Can you imagine any of the women being able to enjoy the movie, feeling derelict in not helping the poor sick children?

Grandma Frances was passive-aggressive at home, too. She went home on a weekend pass, and on returning, she said that she had a very pleasant, enjoyable weekend. The husband reported to the social worker that he had been miserable from the moment she came until the moment she left. When I told my supervisor about this discrepancy, he said, "What discrepancy? The husband said she made him miserable, and she said this was enjoyable. I don't see any discrepancy. She enjoys making people miserable."

Grandma Frances was never aggressive. She did not shout at anyone or act belligerently. But with her quiet way of deflating people's egos and making them feel guilty, she was more aggressive than if she had struck them with a baseball bat.

Passive-aggressive people avoid being assertive. They are often irritable, sulky and resistive. If you ask them to do something, they usually do not refuse, but dilly-dally for so long that you go ahead and do it yourself. Or, they will do what you ask in such a way that you will have to undo it and do it over. They make it impossible for you to criticize them, because they make it seem as though they were doing their very best, and if things did not turn out well, it was your fault for not giving proper instructions. They point out that they are doing the job much better than other people, and nobody appreciates their hard work. They often scorn people in authority and are quick to point out their shortcomings. They may conveniently forget to do what they are asked.

I had a passive-aggressive patient who was adept at cutting people down to size. One time, I prescribed a medication for her, and the following week she reported that my medication had made her very sick. "I asked the druggist for something, and what he gave me made me feel much better." Another patient who was critical of her previous psychiatrist said to me, "I guess you don't understand me any better than anyone else."

When passive-aggressives are assigned a task, they will occupy themselves with minutiae and neglect the important things. They may see every request of them as an imposition. They may complain of physical pains that preclude them from completing the task, thereby increasing the burden on everyone else. They expect you to feel sympathy for them. How can you criticize them when you must feel pity for their suffering?

Passive-aggressives may interpret your orders or suggestions literally, thereby actually being defiant, but in such a way that you are to blame for not being more specific. It is related that the legendary *golem* created by the MaHaral of Prague was told to catch fish. He returned with a huge load of fish. When he was told that was too much, he promptly threw *all* the fish back. Passive-aggressive people often act this way.

With their passive-aggressiveness, these people can wield much control. While they do not overtly refuse to do something, their behavior is such that it becomes easier for you to do what *they* want rather than what you want.

It is easy to fall into the trap of the passive-dependent or passive-aggressive person. There is little you can do to change them. Expert therapy may help, but they are notoriously resistant to therapy, because they do not see anything wrong with their behavior. The best you can do is recognize that they are controlling you and simply not allow yourself to be controlled by them.

The Hillel Formula

There is another control issue of great importance, although it is more subtle. Rather than the problem of wielding control over others, it is adopting a lifestyle in which you *allow yourself to be controlled by others*. It is wise to consider the opinions of others, but in the final analysis, one must be one's own person. *One must have an identity not imposed by others.*

The formula for a healthy adjustment to life and for an identity of one's own was stated by the great sage, Hillel. "If I am not for myself, who will be for me? If I am only for myself, what am I? And if not now, then when?" (*Ethics of the Fathers* 1:14).

Lest one should think that having one's own identity is *gaavah* (vanity) one should know something about the author of this statement.

The Talmud states that Hillel was as deserving of Divine revelation as Moses, but his generation did not merit having it (*Sanhedrin* 11a). Throughout the Talmud, the law almost always follows the opinion of the school which he founded.

Hillel's humility is legendary. His sensitivity to the dignity of others is demonstrated by the incident where he bought a horse for a prominent person who had fallen upon bad times, and because there was no servant to run before him and announce his coming as he was accustomed to in his affluent days, Hillel personally ran before him (*Kesubos* 67b).

Hillel's tolerance and patience were limitless. The Talmud relates that someone made a wager that he could provoke Hillel to rage, and he continually pestered Hillel at the most inopportune times with the most ridiculous questions. To each of these foolish questions, Hillel responded respectfully, "You have asked a very good question, my child," and then proceeded to answer it.

Hillel's teachings are the fundamentals of Jewish ethics.

"Do not separate yourself from the community; do not believe in yourself until the day you die; do not judge your fellow until you have reached his place; do not make a statement that cannot be easily understood on the ground that it will be understood eventually; and do not say, 'When I am free I will study,' for perhaps you may not become free" (*Ethics of the Fathers* 2:5).

"Be among the disciples of Aaron, loving peace and pursuing peace, loving people and bringing them closer to Torah" (ibid. 1:12).

"He who seeks renown loses his reputation...and he who exploits the crown of Torah shall fade away" (ibid. 2:13).

"In a place where there are no leaders, strive to be a leader" (ibid. 2:6).

"When I am humble, I am elevated. When I elevate myself, I am lowered" (*Vayikra Rabbah* 1).

The Talmud relates incidents of Hillel's life which indicate that he lived according to his teachings. With all this as a background, we can now turn to a statement of Hillel which will shed light on his "formula." "At the celebration of the Succos festival, Hillel said, 'If I am here, then all is here. If I am not here, who then is here?'" (*Succah* 53).

How is it possible that someone of unparalleled humility and self-effacement should say, "If I am here, then all is here?"

I believe that Hillel was referring to having an identity of his own, rather than being dependent on others to define him. That Hillel advocates this should eliminate any concern that having one's own identity is in any way related to vanity.

The Chassidic master, R' Mendel of Kotzk, said, "If I am I because I am I, and you are you because you are you, then *I am I* and *you are you*. But, if I am I *because* you are you, and you are you *because* I am I, then *I am not I* and *you are not you*." This is a rather colorful way of saying that if a person lacks an identity of his own and is dependent on what others think of him for his identity, then he in fact does not have an identity.

Some people's lives are totally regulated by approval-seeking and people-pleasing. This is because they believe, consciously or subconsciously, that they can be loved, accepted and respected *only* if they do what they think others want or expect them to do. They may be totally preoccupied with making sure that they do "the right thing," and their idea of "the right thing" is not what is inherently right, but what other people think is right.

What does this have to do with control? *Without a personal identity, a person sees the real control over his life as being from external sources rather than from inner sources.* This person can never "be himself" because he has no self. He is only what he thinks others want him to be.

As was noted, people may resent being controlled. The person who allows others to control him may actually build up resentments against the people whom he purportedly loves.

Doing things for others can be of two types: *chesed* and people-pleasing. The behavior may appear similar, but people-pleasing is as different from *chesed* as fool's gold is from real gold.

Hillel's *chesed* is exemplary. Hillel did not run as a servant before the coach of the erstwhile affluent person because he wished to ingratiate himself with him. Indeed, this was an act of *chesed* which is not expected of anyone. Hillel did so out of the conviction that doing a kindness for a person is a mitzvah, even if the kind act may appear to be absurd.

People-pleasing is not a pure mitzvah. It is a self-serving maneuver directed toward acquiring someone's affection or friendship. The people-pleaser tries to control other people's behavior toward him by what he does for them. This results in an entanglement, in that he tries to control others' reactions while he is, in a way, being controlled by them.

I must share with you a personal experience. Earlier in my life, I was preoccupied with what others thought of me. I was a people-pleaser *par excellence*. I tried to acquire the respect and affection of others by what I did for them.

If someone asked me to do something for him, I promptly agreed, not because it was the right thing to do, but because I was afraid to alienate him by refusing. I felt trapped. Although I did many favors, I often resented doing them. I would do them at the expense of attention I should have been giving to my family. I resented people imposing upon me because I was powerless to refuse them. I was angry at myself for not having the strength to refuse an improper request. Doing *chesed* should result in a good feeling, and not in anger at the whole world.

As I gained in self-awareness and self-esteem, I was able to relinquish this "people-pleasing" behavior. Today I am free to turn down certain requests, and when I do *chesed*, I thoroughly enjoy doing a mitzvah.

Hillel's statement, "If I am not for myself, who will be for me?" is a lucid expression of the identity issue. "If I do not have an identity of my own, then no one can give me one. I can be like a chameleon, changing appearances with every environment. If I am an approval-seeking people-pleaser, then I have no identity." This is also what R' Mendel of Kotzk meant.

But having an identity of one's own does not mean that one should be self-centered. To the contrary, one is then able to do true *chesed*. This is the second part of Hillel's statement, "If I am only for myself, what am I?" I may have an identity, but of what use am I to the world?

A person with an inner identity who is not totally dependent on what others think of him can give serious consideration to other people's opinions, and weigh the pros and cons objectively. Someone whose identity depends on what others think of him is likely to react by either adopting others' opinions out of his fear to disagree, or reject them out of hand because he feels he is being manipulated.

It is interesting that in the many *halachic* disputes between the schools of Hillel and Shammai, the Talmud generally accepts the ruling of the school of Hillel, because "they were humble, and they always cited the Shammai school opinion before their own" (*Eruvin* 13b). The school of Hillel had adopted an inner identity as did their founder, which allowed them to give proper consideration to a dissenting opinion.

A person with an inner identity can initiate action. A person dependent on others for his identity can only *react*. He bases his opinion on what others think.

"If I am here, all is here" is a corollary to the Hillel formula. It simply means that if I have an identity of my own, then all of me is in fact here. "If I am not here," i.e., if I do not have an identity of my own, then who is it that is here? What you see here is not really me. It is merely a shadow, a reflection of everyone else. I can be one person at one time and place and a totally different person at another time and place.

The Talmud says that "the pursuit of renown removes a person from the world" (*Ethics of the Fathers* 4:28). Pursuit of renown is a desperate attempt to acquire an identity via being acknowledged by other people. It "removes a person from the world" because it is an attempt to fill a bottomless pit. An identity based on acclaim is fragile and ephemeral. It lasts only for the duration of the acclaim. When the latter is over, the person falls back into a distressing feeling of nothingness.

I recall a man who vociferously demanded that he be given the first *hakaffah* (procession with the Torah) on Simchas Torah. He was humored because the officers of the shul wished to avoid his ire. He was not respected. To the contrary, he was resented because of his attitude. He did wield control by virtue of his unpleasant personality. The feelings toward him are typical of those toward anyone who wields control. It is also obvious that this person's self-esteem was so low that he had to insist on being recognized. What was his identity? He was known as an unpleasant person to whom you had to relate with great caution in order to avoid saying or doing something which he might consider offensive.

Identity and control are closely related issues. With an inner identity, one has a self-esteem that does not necessitate dominating others in order to have a feeling of self-worth, nor does one allow oneself to be controlled by others.

The Undeveloped Self

Controlling others and allowing oneself to be controlled by others are generally both the result of the failure of an inner identity. In the former, a person tries to compensate for a lack of an inner identity by assuming the position, "I am the boss," whether this be parent, teacher, police officer, employer or any one else in a position of authority. Inasmuch as he lacks an inner "I am," he adopts an external identity, "I am the boss." In the latter, the person assumes the identity others impose upon him.

It is difficult for a person to live without a sense of "I am." In desperation, a person may accept a negative identity if he feels he cannot have any other. Some people have even chosen the identity of being an addict or a criminal. Any identity is better than none at all.

Why do so many people fail to develop an inner identity? Why do they become controllers or subject themselves to being controlled? My mother commented on the verse in *Psalms* (90:14), "Satisfy us in the morning with Your kindness, then we shall sing out and rejoice throughout our days." Inasmuch as the latter half of the verse, "throughout our days," refers to all of one's life, what is meant by "satisfy us in the morning?" She said that it can only mean "in the morning *of our lives*," i.e., as children. The psalmist is saying that if a child's needs are satisfied in the dawn of life, he can be happy throughout his life.

Earlier, I alluded to the importance of addressing a child's needs. Let me elaborate a bit on this important topic.

For any of many reasons, a child's needs may not be satisfied. In many instances, the parents are *not at fault*, even though they may have failed to satisfy a child's needs. Let me explain.

A mother develops a chronic, disabling illness which makes it impossible for her to care for her child. The father must work to support the family. They may do their utmost to see that the child gets the best care possible, but it just does not satisfy the child's needs. No one is *at fault*, but the child's needs are not met. Or, perhaps both parents must work to meet the family's economic needs. Again, there may not be enough time or energy to meet the child's needs.

Even in situations where both parents are available to the child, *they may not be able to give the child what they do not have.* "He visits the sins of the parents on the children and on the children's children" (*Exodus* 34:7). This is equally true of emotional deficiencies. Generations of Jews have lived under circumstances of deprivation and persecution. Their emotional well-being was curtailed, and even when conditions improved, their own stunted emotional development precluded their being able to satisfy their children's needs. Again, no one is to be blamed, but the child's needs are nevertheless not met.

I have seen situations where a woman described the lack of her childhood needs being met, and saying, "I will never do to my children what my mother did to me." Yet, it is predictable that most often they will relate to their children *exactly* the way their parents related to them. Why? Because that is all they know how to do.

Most parents have good intentions and wish the best for their children. Unfortunately, they may not be able to deliver. *The greatest emotional trauma a child can experience is the frustration of his desire to feel that he matters and that he can be loved and accepted as a person, unconditionally.* Unconditional love is not pampering.

Children are naturally dependent. As infants, they are not able to express their needs and may not even know what their needs are. Parents have the responsibility of trying to understand what the child needs and provide for it. Let me reiterate. Parents who, as children, did not have their own needs met may be at a disadvantage in understanding their child.

We have heard horror stories of parents who have killed their children by shaking them violently because they would not stop crying. While this is indeed rare, it is not uncommon for a parent to be very irritated by a child who continues crying, and say in exasperation, "I don't know what that child wants!" If the parent is completely honest, he/she would admit feeling angry at the child for incessantly crying. Under the best circumstances, it may not be possible for a parent to know the child's needs. It may also be, however, that the parent may lack the sensitivity to understand the child's needs.

(Note: I think it is a bit awkward to always say he/she, him/her or his/hers. I'm going to say either "he," "him" and "his," or "she," "her" and "hers" and I depend upon you to realize that this applies both ways.)

Psychologists speak about the "inner child." We all begin life as infants and advance through many stages as we grow into adulthood. If each stage is navigated satisfactorily, we progress to the next stage without any negative baggage. If we advance to the next developmental level without having properly completed a previous level, we may take the unfinished business along with us.

Our conscious minds can operate with intellect and rational thinking. We mature primarily in our conscious mind. Our *subconscious* mind is totally different. It may not mature as we grow older. It can retain memories and emotions for decades, and does not operate under rules of rationality. A highly intelligent person of sixty may react emotionally as a three-year-old.

The "inner child" refers to those feelings and ideas which were not dealt with adequately in childhood, and which may linger on throughout adult life. This is why intelligent parents may react inappropriately to their children. Their reactions may be influenced by "inner child" feelings.

Children have very strong emotions. These can be nurtured or repressed by parents. Children whose parents react negatively to their crying may learn not to cry. There are parents who may discourage children from laughing. These children may have stunted emotions as they grow up, and when they become parents, they may react to their children with stunted emotions.

Play is a natural component of life. You may have seen videos of young animals who engage in play. Certainly, children have a need to play, even when they are beyond the toddler stage. Some adults may not appreciate this.

One of my favorite stories was related to me by a rabbi who studied in the Lubavitcher Yeshivah in Brooklyn in the 1940's. He was playing ball with his friends in front of the yeshivah on Eastern Parkway, when their instructor came out and took the ball away from them, reprimanding them for playing ball instead of studying Talmud. When the instructor left, a ball was thrown to them from the second floor window. Looking up, they saw the smiling face of the previous Lubavitcher Rebbe, R' Yosef Yitzchok. The Rebbe understood what the instructor did not.

In order to have a sense of self, a person must be aware of his uniqueness. Torah literature tells us that each *neshamah* (soul) comes into the world with a very specific mission. No other person, not even the combined totality of all humans throughout history, can fulfill the particular purpose of a given *neshamah*. A child should begin to feel this uniqueness.

Parents who are wrapped up in their own emotional problems may not be able to provide for their child's emotional needs. Again, the parent may not be *at fault*, but the child's needs remain unfulfilled.

A person can develop a sense of self only if he feels unique, rather than being just a part of an amorphous humanity, community or family.

How careful our Torah personalities were in giving children a sense of worth! The psalmist says, "From the mouths of infants and sucklings You have established strength" (*Psalms* 8:3), and the Talmud (*Shabbos* 119b) states that the world exists in "the merit of the breath of children." There are accounts of how they would listen thoughtfully to a *berachah* recited by a child and answer with a spirited *Amen*. Parents should concentrate on ways to convey to each child his importance and uniqueness.

It is understandable that parents may see their children as extensions of themselves, but children must be allowed and helped to feel themselves to be individuals. A parent may say to a child, "I know you better than you know yourself." If the child believes that, he may not believe that he has a self except as the parent sees him.

A couple took their six-year-old son with them to a restaurant. The waitress took the parents' orders, then turned to the child. "What will you have, young man?" she said.

The child said, "Two hot dogs with lots of mustard and a Coke."

The mother smiled at the waitress and said, "You can bring him some roast beef and vegetables."

A bit later, the waitress brought the parents' orders, and in front of the child she placed two hot dogs and a Coke. The mother was horrified, but the child grinned from ear to ear and said, "Look, Mom. She thinks I'm real."

If children are completely controlled by parents, they may never develop a sense of being a self in their own right.

When children reach the age when they can participate in household chores, they should indeed do so. However, this should be fair and with consideration of the child's abilities and needs. Children are sometimes unfairly burdened by unrealistic demands.

Evelyn is a woman whose mother was emotionally unable to care for her children. At age eight, Evelyn was doing the diapers and looking after her younger siblings. She essentially became a mother at age eight! She never developed a sense of self. From her earliest days, she was only someone who cared for others. Her own needs were unmet. In fact, she did not even know that she had any needs.

Evelyn raised her children and cared for her sick husband. When he died and she had no one to care for, her "inner child" emerged in full force, and she controlled her children with an insatiable neediness.

Evelyn was not a bad woman. She was a desperate woman, as desperate as a person with a parched throat thirsting for water in an arid desert.

Needs are needs. Because we have all been thirsty at times, we can empathize with a very thirsty person. Emotional needs are as real as the need for water. Evelyn's emotional thirst resulting from the gross deprivation of her childhood needs surfaced after her husband's death. She used her loneliness as a means to control her children, with constant, unrealistic demands on them. Evelyn's children's love for her was marred by the increasing resentments of her imposition on them.

Evelyn's daughter-in-law could not tolerate the incessant demands on her husband that took him away from her and their children. When the husband was unable to free himself from Evelyn's control, the wife's patience was finally exhausted and she filed for divorce.

This is an example of the evil of control.

There are marriages where a spouse does not meet the partner's needs. A husband or wife may turn to a son or daughter to provide the companionship, affection or intellectual stimulation that is lacking from the partner. Although there may not be the slightest hint of any meanness, this demand on a child may constitute emotional abuse. Whenever a child is expected to provide that which a spouse is lacking, the potential for emotional abuse exists.

If we recall our childhood days, we will remember how cruel kids can be. Children may be made fun of because they are poor, fat, not athletic, have a speech or physical defect or are not bright. This can cause deep hurt. Parents should be aware of their children's sensitivities and problems at school, and when necessary, get expert advice on how to help the child.

How wise my mother's interpretation of the verse in *Psalms* was! "Satisfy us in the morning with Your kindness, then we shall sing out and rejoice throughout our days." If a child's needs are satisfied in the dawn of life, he can be happy throughout his life.

Coping with Controlling People

n any relationship—parent/child, teacher/student, husband/wife, employer/employee, doctor/patient, lawyer/client or even friend/friend—there is always the possibility of control. Just walking away from a controlling person is not an ideal solution and not always feasible nor desirable. We need to learn how to best cope with controlling people. We will analyze several relationships and give some suggestions that may help one to cope. There are a few general principles that apply to all relationships.

When someone tries to control you, you may either *respond* or *react*. These two terms are anything but similar. Responding can be positive, whereas reacting is usually negative. We can see the difference even in our everyday language. For example, your doctor has prescribed a medication for you. On a subsequent visit he says, "You are *responding* very well to the medication." On the other hand, if you break out with hives or a rash, the doctor says, "You've had a *reaction* to the medication." "Response" means that your body has absorbed it and it is doing its thing. "Reaction" means that the body is rejecting the medication.

We speak of a "knee-jerk *reaction*." The connotation is that the person is reacting spontaneously and immediately, just as the foot kicks when the knee is tapped. Physiologically, the knee-jerk reaction takes place in the spinal cord. It does not go up to the brain. That is what most reactions are: no-brainers. Response means that you have absorbed the other person's idea, processed it through your brain, and are coming back with a well thought-out response.

Don't *react* to a controlling person. Think and *respond.*

Being interrupted before you finish what you want to say is very irritating. If you *respond*, you will hear the person out. That is respectful and will be appreciated. If you *react* without thinking, you are apt to do so before the person has finished his sentence. Not only is this rude, but you may also be jumping to a false conclusion and reacting defensively to what you *think* the person is going to say. You may be mistaken. You stand to gain by avoiding reacting.

After you have heard what the other person says, you may say, "Correct me if I'm wrong. What I understand from you is...." Sometimes, the person may say, "That's not what I meant." Even if he says brusquely, "Exactly!" you've lost nothing. Furthermore, you've assured him that you've heard him. That makes it easier to say, "O.K., I hear your point. I want to think it over a bit." Then you can *respond.*

As was noted, a controlling person sometimes acts that way because controlling others gives him an ego boost and builds up his lagging self-esteem. What if you're able to say something that builds up his self-esteem? He may just not have quite as much need to control. This may not always work, but it's worth trying.

I don't mean you should be fawning. Giving false compliments is disgusting. But you should be able to find something about the person that is praiseworthy. For example, a response to your boss who is critical of something you did may be, "I've got to admit, Mr. Jones, you sure do run a tight ship! If I ever get to be in a similar position, I'll probably do the same thing." You might not like what he said, but he probably is running a tight ship and he may appreciate that it is recognized.

I do not intend to make this a book on "how to win friends and influence people." By the way, there is a classic book by that very title, written by Dale Carnegie many years ago, and it has really not been improved upon. Do yourself a great favor and read it. It never hurts to learn better ways to communicate. Nevertheless, I do want to make a suggestion or two.

If you have read some of my other writings, you know that I'm hooked on the theme of self-esteem, and as I've just said, whatever you can do to elevate a person's self-esteem can be helpful in any relationship.

You are a new son-in-law or daughter-in-law. Yes, we have heard much about difficulties in in-law relationships and we will discuss them a bit later. These difficulties generally do not ensue from day one.

You may be able to head off some problems or to at least mitigate them by saying right at the beginning, perhaps even the first chance you get to talk to them after the *chuppah*, "I want to thank you for having raised your daughter to be such a wonderful wife." That is not a false compliment. You married your wife because you had reason to believe that she is a good person. She did not grow up like a weed. Parents invest considerable energy in raising their children. You will thank people who give you a wedding gift. Your in-laws invested much effort in the gift they have given you, and this should be acknowledged and appreciated. It certainly will not hurt your relationship to repeat this expression of gratitude. It will raise their self-esteem for having done a good job in parenting. They may also confide in your wife, "You know what Shmuli said to us? He thanked us for having raised such a wonderful person to be his wife. That was so thoughtful and sweet of him."

If you are the parent-in-law, you may also say, right from the start, "We are so happy to have you as a son-in-law. We know that Estee is going to be very happy with you." People often live up to what is expected of them.

Whenever you wish to communicate a criticism of any kind in a relationship, *begin with something positive.* The Torah teaches this in *Deuteronomy* 28. The reward of blessings precedes the harsh warning of punishment.

You should be able to find something praiseworthy in every person. If you cannot, perhaps you are not looking well enough for it. In the beautiful "prayer before prayer" composed by R' Elimelech of Lizhensk, he says, "Help me see the good in other people, not their faults." The Torah says, "G-d will bless you in all *that you do*" (*Deuteronomy* 14:29). If you wish G-d to answer this prayer, you should begin by looking for the good in every person.

President Lincoln once said, "I don't like that man very much. I'm going to have to get to know him better." This is a very wise statement, indicating that our dislike of a person may be because we know him only superficially. It is surprising what good we may discover in a person.

One of my childhood memories is a squabble that occurred between a famous *chazan* (cantor) and the shul that had engaged him for the High Holidays. The shul had overestimated their income, and, several days before Rosh Hashanah, when the *chazan* came to Milwaukee he was told that they were unable to pay him the sum they had promised, and would he please agree upon a lesser amount. The *chazan* was furious, and he brought the shul officers to my father with his complaint. "It is not my worry how the shul gets its money," he said to my father. "A contract is a contract. I will not lower my price by even a nickel. Furthermore, I now want the entire amount placed with you in escrow, otherwise they can find someone else to *daven* (lead the services)."

On Erev Rosh Hashanah the officers came to my father and gave him a sum of money. "This is all we have," they said. "Perhaps you can prevail upon him to *daven* anyway."

My father called in the *chazan*, and no sooner had he uttered the words, "The shul officers were here…" than the *chazan* interrupted him. "Rebbe," he said, "how can you talk to me today about money? It's Erev Rosh Hashanah. I didn't give G-d all I had promised Him either. I'm *davening!*"

Nu, should we judge a person by first impressions? If we get to know a person better, we are certain to find things about him that are praiseworthy. If you assume someone is an ogre, he is likely to act like one.

Someone said to me, "The proverb that 'You can catch more bees with honey than you can with vinegar' is so true. How come that's not in the Bible?"

I said, "Of course it is. Solomon said, 'A soft response turns away wrath' (*Proverbs* 15:1). This is a basic rule of communication."

President Lincoln is credited with the tactic of first presenting the other side's position in any disagreement. It is said that when he addressed a jury, he would say, "Here are the facts my learned opponent presents." He did this so convincingly that an observer might have thought he was representing the other side! He would then go on to present his case. The implication to the jury was, "I'm trying to be as honest and fair as possible."

This is an excellent tactic, but it predated Lincoln by two thousand years. As was mentioned earlier, the Talmud says that there were many disagreements between the schools of Hillel and Shammai, and that Hillel school's position was nearly always accepted as the *halachah*. Why is this so? Because "they were not only humble, *but they presented the opinion of the Shammai school before their own*" (*Eruvin* 13b).

In coping with a person who wants to tell you what to do, you can apply this principle by saying, "I know what you want me to do, and I can see your points in why you want it that way. But allow me to think about it first, O.K.?" Again, this may not always work, but it is often successful. You have elevated the person's self-esteem by granting that he has good reasons for his request. If you *react* by saying, "No way!" or "That's absurd!" or any similar negative comment, you have attacked the person's self-esteem by implying that he is unfair or that he does not know what he is talking about. That is apt to reinforce the person's need to be controlling.

Here is another suggestion to boost self-esteem, or at least not to depress self-esteem. This is simple courtesy toward everyone, but especially important in relating to a controlling person. In a telephone conversation, *hang up last*. You know what it feels like when immediately after the last word was said you hear a click. "That person was too quick to hang up. Obviously, he couldn't wait to get off the phone with me." You don't want to give a controller a reason to feel you are rejecting him, so wait until the other party hangs up first. In those instances where I was too quick to hang up, I immediately call back the other person and say, "I'm sorry. I didn't mean to hang up on you." This may sound picayune, but you will be surprised how such a minor thing can be important.

I do not know why this is, but when we are in a face-to-face conversation and the phone rings, we tend to answer the phone. Why does the caller have priority over the person with whom you are conversing face-to-face? It is actually a kind of insult to answer the phone, and if your face-to-face person is a controller, you have aggravated the situation. Let your answering machine take the call. This tells the person with whom you are talking that you value the conversation.

If I am expecting a very important call, I tell the person before we begin our conversation, "I'm expecting a very important call that I can't afford to miss. I will have to answer the phone if it rings. I hope you won't mind." If the caller is not the important call you're expecting, promptly say, "I'm sorry, but I'm with someone now. Please give me your number and I'll call you when I'm free," or, "You may call me back in an hour." Again, this tells the person that you value the conversation with him.

One of the steps prescribed in the recovery program for alcoholics is "when wrong, promptly admit it." This is a most valuable habit to develop for every person, not only an alcoholic. There is a natural tendency to defend a mistake. Don't do it! Be big enough to admit you may have been wrong. Apologizing does not lower your self-esteem. On the contrary, it elevates it. At the same time, it also elevates the self-esteem of the person to whom you apologized. Apology is a win-win act.

The alcoholism recovery program adds an important feature: "When wrong, *promptly* admit it." Some people try to cover up a mistake and admit it only when there is "smoking gun" evidence of it. This is a serious error which toppled a president of the United States from office and almost toppled a second president. Don't be defensive. It is O.K. to make a mistake. Human beings are fallible. It is not O.K. to deny it. The sooner you admit it, the quicker an argument is put to rest and the more your stature rises in the eyes of others.

It is a natural human tendency to want to be the winner. When two people disagree, each one wants to win. Remember, what you should be interested in is a proper solution to the issue at hand. You have read this book, but the other person may not have read it, so you are better equipped. *Focus on finding the best solution, not on winning the argument.*

The Torah says, "Do not accept a bribe" (*Deuteronomy* 16:19). This applies to every person, not only to magistrates. We all make many judgments each day, so in a sense we are all judges and we should not allow ourselves to be bribed.

A bribe is not only graft. When a decision can go either way and one of them is more pleasant and desirable, that constitutes a bribe. You are bribed by what is most desirable for you.

The Torah says that "a bribe blinds the eyes of the wise and distorts the words of the righteous" (ibid.). You may be a very wise and decent person, but you are not immune to the blinding and distorting effects of a bribe.

The desire to come out the winner in a dispute is a bribe. Even if your opponent's position is the correct one, you may not be able to see it that way, because your perception has been blocked and your judgment has been distorted.

Let's take a hypothetical case. Your wife just gave birth to a baby girl, and everyone is happy. Now comes the choice of a name. You want to name her after someone in your family, and your wife's parents want her to be named after someone in their family. A silly argument? Of course. But such silly arguments have been the beginning of family troubles.

It is conceivable that your in-laws' reasons for their position may be valid. There already is a name in your family for your grandmother, but there is as yet no name for your father-in-law's mother. If you were able to perceive correctly and judge properly, you might recognize that they are right. However, your emotional ties to your beloved grandmother are a bribe. You *want* that name. In addition, your desire to come out the winner in the dispute is another bribe. You may be incapable of making a proper judgment. You see your in-laws' position as being meddling and an attempt to control. This may not be true, but your "bribes" make you see it that way.

This holds true for every dispute. The only way to avoid unnecessary trouble is to make a conscious effort to quash your desire to be the winner. Try your utmost to set that desire aside. Say to yourself, "I don't have to win. The issue should be decided on its merits." If you can overcome the natural desire to win, you may get along much more easily, even with a controlling person.

Accepting a valid decision, even from a "control freak," does not mean you are surrendering to control. Sticking to your guns and refusing to accept a proper decision just because the other person is a controller is being obstinate.

A bit of clarification is in order. The Talmud says that a person should always be flexible and not be obstinate (*Taanis* 20b). This does not mean that one must always yield to another person's wish.

There is a difference whether a person acts on intellect or on emotion. Emotions are not reliable, and may cause a person to do wrong. If a parent disciplines a child because the child must learn right from wrong, that is good. If he does so because he is angry at the child for doing something and acts out his anger, that is bad. The actual behavior may be identical in both cases, but whether it is good or bad is determined by the reason for the behavior.

Proper discipline is determined by the intellect. Reacting in anger is an emotional discharge.

A person may yield to the opinion of a control freak because he has come around to realize that it is in fact the right decision. If he yields because he is emotionally unable to assert himself properly, that is not good for him nor for the control freak, whose urge to control is reinforced by the other person's passivity. The Talmudic statement that a person should always be flexible does not mean that one should be passive. A flexible rod is one that *can* be bent, not one that *is* bent. Being flexible means *being able* to accept another person's differing viewpoint when it is correct. This requires a dispassionate and objective judgment. Inasmuch as one may not always be able to be dispassionate and objective, it is wise to consult a disinterested person whenever possible.

Obstinacy and passivity are extremes. Rambam says that we should avoid extremes and choose a median position between the two.

Very often, people will live up to your expectations of them. If you have pegged someone as being a control freak and relate to him based on that assumption, you may well make him into a control freak. If you see him as a rational person who will listen to reason *when properly approached*, he is more likely to do just that.

Control Issues
in Marriage

One of the areas where control can wreak havoc and cause extreme harm is in the marriage relationship. A happy, successful marriage is a harmonious relationship between the two partners. *Any power struggle undermines the foundation of a marriage.*

Torah is most emphatic about respect for others. There are even instances where preserving a person's honor may override a Torah prohibition. The Talmud says, "Your student's honor should be as dear to you as your own, and your friend's honor should be as dear to you as your teacher's" (*Ethics of the Fathers* 4:15). The importance of upholding a person's dignity can be seen from the

Talmudic statement that "if one humiliates a person publicly, even if he is a Torah scholar and has many mitzvos, he forfeits his portion in the World to Come" (Ibid. 3:15). The Chafetz Chaim says that this holds true even if the humiliation occurs in private. This punishment of forfeiting one's portion in the World to Come is most grave, and is not mentioned even in regard to major Scriptural transgressions.

Human dignity is of unparalleled importance. *Nowhere is there an exemption if the other person is one's spouse.* To the contrary, the Talmud says that a husband should "love his wife as he loves himself, and respect her *even more* than he respects himself" (*Yevamos* 62b).

Trying to control another person is degrading and belittling. This is true especially when that person is one's spouse. Exerting power over a husband or wife is a serious transgression of Torah.

The severity of this transgression is multiplied many times when the offended person has no recourse for help. The Torah decrees the harshest of punishments for anyone who torments a widow or orphan (*Exodus* 22:21), and Rashi states that this is equally true for any person who is essentially helpless.

There are marriages where circumstances enable a spouse to wield power over the partner. As was noted earlier, control breeds resentment, not love. One cannot love a tyrant. A spouse who exerts control over the partner should know that he is crushing the love the other person had for him.

In the traditional Jewish family, the husband was the breadwinner and the wife was the homemaker. Inasmuch as the husband had primary access to the family income, he could exert control by making the wife totally dependent on him for money. In today's economy, this occurs if the wife cannot sign a check or have a credit card. Putting the wife on a weekly allowance as one would do with a juvenile is an affront to her dignity. The reverse is true when the wife supplies the family income, either by her earnings or her family's support. If she utilizes this to control the husband, this is both a transgression and an undermining of the marriage relationship.

The reason that control is so frequent in marriage is because the home may be the only place a spouse may feel that he can be in control. People who feel controlled at work or by others in any way may see the home as the only place they can exert power, and they take advantage of it.

A spouse may be acting out of deep-seated anxiety and insecurity. For example, a husband who objects to his wife going out with her female friends may feel that she enjoys their company more than his. "If she likes them so much, what place do I occupy in this relationship?" This is particularly true of people with poor self-esteem who doubt that they are lovable. He may also feel that her friends are influencing her in a way that is contrary to his wishes.

The following case is an example of how poor self-esteem may result in an attempt to control.

Gladys consulted me because she was afraid that her marriage was falling apart. Ed had always been a kind and considerate person, but had recently undergone a radical change. He was cantankerous and trying to control her every move. She could not understand what had gotten into him.

When I saw Ed, the following emerged. Ed and Gladys had been happily married for seventeen years and had three children. Ed was a contractor who built homes. When the youngest child was in school for a full day, Gladys found too much time on her hands, and decided to take a course in real-estate, resulting in her becoming a licensed realtor. Ed had encouraged this, reasoning that it would complement his contracting business.

After Gladys succeeded in selling several homes and earning a commission, Ed's attitude changed. He resented her work. If she wanted to show a home in the evening, he would say, "You shouldn't be going out at night. It's too dangerous." If she wanted to show a home on a weekend, he would say, "This is the only time you have to spend with the children. You shouldn't be away from home when the kids are home." On several deals he tried to "help" Gladys, and managed to sabotage the deal.

I found that Ed had such poor self-esteem that he did not think he was lovable. He was insecure in having Gladys' love. As long as he was the sole income producer, he was secure in the marriage because he felt that Gladys was dependent on him economically. However, if she was capable of supporting herself, what was there to keep her tied to him? Her ability to earn was very threatening to him.

Ed entered group therapy, eventually overcoming his distorted self-concept, and realized that Gladys did indeed love him. He was then able to relinquish control. Ironically, his attempt to control Gladys in order to keep her in the marriage could have had the opposite effect. Gladys might not have been able to stay in a marriage where her husband wielded total control.

Spouses who doubt that they can be loved may try to put the partner through tests to prove that they indeed love them. "If she really loves me, she will give in and do what I say." They may have no awareness that this is what they are doing.

What can one do if one feels controlled by a spouse?

Perhaps the first thing to do is to take a look at yourself. Sometimes a spouse's control is a reaction, a kind of tug-of-war. If you feel your husband is controlling, try to see, "Is there anything I may be doing to exert control over him in any way?" It is conceivable that he may be trying to control because he feels that *you* are controlling.

Do you insist on going to your parents for Shabbos when he would rather be at home?

Do you take his wishes into consideration? No, I am not trying to find excuses to justify a husband's control, but this is something that must be considered.

If you feel that control is a problem, *don't sweep it under the rug.* Trying to keep peace in the marriage by ignoring problems is unwise. Over time, control may escalate until it becomes intolerable, resulting in serious threats to the relationship. It is much easier to deal with the problem in its earliest stages. Bring the issue out in the open.

"Honey, I don't want anything to spoil our relationship. If I can't sign checks or have a credit card, I am dependent on the money you give me every week. Even if it is enough, the feeling that this gives me is that I am a child being given an allowance. It is not a good feeling, and I don't want to have anything but positive feelings toward you. If you see me spending money unwisely, tell me about it. I'm happy to listen to your opinion, but I can't stand being treated like a juvenile."

Or, "Honey, I know you resent my going out with my friends. I love you and I love our home, but I do need some time with my friends. When you go to any of your activities, I don't see it as being a sign that you don't love me. I know you love me and that you may need some 'alone time' or being with your friends. I want you to feel the same about me."

Many spouses may be unaware that they are in a power struggle. Here is a simple exercise. Whenever there is a difference of opinion about something, *write down whose opinion prevailed.* This should include even minutiae. The husband chose a tie. The wife says, "No, that tie doesn't go with that suit."

"But I happen to like it."

"It looks weird. People will wonder why I let you go out like that."

"That's my problem, not yours. I'll tell everyone that I chose the tie."

A silly argument? Of course. But many disagreements are not of more substance than this. Whatever the disagreement, write it down and note whose decision prevailed.

Make a list of these incidents and then read it together. You may laugh at some things you disagreed about that were not worth arguing about. You may also discover that an inordinate amount of decisions were made by one of the partners. This may bring the control issue out into the open.

Make a list of your respective strengths, and define your roles. The wife is a better vacation planner. The husband is better at balancing the checkbook. The wife has a better sense of direction. The husband is a better driver. Look at those areas in which each of you is best. This does not have to be cast in concrete, but defining roles and agreeing that each one should do what one is best at can prevent arguments.

Important! Make an agreement to disagree fairly. In politics, candidates pledge to stick to the issues, but the campaign may deteriorate to mud-slinging. Do not be like politicians. Stick to the issues!

You happen to be disagreeing on something. "You're just like your mother, always wanting your way!" That has nothing to do with the issue at hand. "Why do we always have to do things your way?" That may be a valid point for discussion, but has no bearing on the particular object of this disagreement. "Last time we did it your way, and remember the fiasco that resulted?" Even if true, that does not speak to the present decision.

Stick to the issues! No name calling! Promise each other to stick to the issues and avoid any and every kind of personal attack.

Don't make winning an argument an ego issue. Deal with the issues for what they are, and get your pride out of the way.

Incidentally, one man told me what brought peace into their marriage. "I didn't want to lose an argument," he said. "But then I realized that if I won, that meant that she lost. I didn't want to be married to a loser. So we stopped fighting about things and began discussing them on their merits."

Sometimes it's wise to yield in this way:

Husband: "For heaven's sake, don't drive so close to the car ahead of you. You may not be able to stop in time and you'll hit him!"

You can say, "Stop telling me how to drive." Or, you might pull over to the curb at the first opportunity, get out of the car and hand him the keys and say, "O.K., you do the driving." Surprising how this technique works.

Make an agreement to negotiate and compromise. Marriage should not be seen as a struggle to see who will win.

If things do not seem to be working out well, *seek competent counseling*. Find a counselor with established competence in marriage problems. It is not necessary for both partners to go. Seek guidance for yourself. Our best intentions for coping with a controlling person may backfire. Expert advice is invaluable.

Remember Solomon's wise words. "The way of a fool is straight in his own eyes, but he who listens to advice is wise" (*Proverbs* 12:15). There are many reasons why we may not be able to see a situation correctly, and we may react in a counterproductive manner. A wise person seeks counsel. Be wise!

Someone may say, "Why is it wrong for a husband to exert control over his wife? Does not the Torah say that because Eve disobeyed Him, she was punished that 'he (the husband) shall rule over you' (*Genesis* 3:16)?"

There was a sect known as Karaites that took everything in the Torah literally. They would punish a person who blinded someone by blinding him because the Torah says, "An eye for an eye." They sat in darkness all Shabbos because the Torah says, "Do not kindle a flame in your homes on Shabbos." The Karaites ate meat with milk because the Torah only says, "You shall not cook a kid in its mother's milk." We follow the Torah as interpreted by the Talmud. Let us see what the Talmud says about the husband/wife relationship.

We have already noted the Talmudic statement that a husband should "love his wife as he loves himself, and respect her *even more* than he respects himself" (*Yevamos* 62b). Dominating a wife is not according her the respect that the Talmud requires. Rav says that a husband should be most cautious not to aggrieve his wife, because a woman is emotionally sensitive and is easily moved to tears. Causing a wife emotional pain will bring swift Divine punishment (*Bava Metzia* 59a). Incidentally, the Talmud says that Rav did not have a good marriage, and that his wife regularly provoked him (*Yevamos* 63a). Yet he is the author of the statement that a husband must not aggrieve his wife! The Talmud also states that a husband should be meticulous in according his wife proper respect, because "the blessing of the household is by the virtue of the wife" (*Bava Metzia* 59a).

Rambam rules that a husband must speak gently to his wife, and should be neither tense nor short-tempered (*Hilchos Ishus* 15:19). Maharal states that precisely because the husband is the head of the household, he must be deeply attuned to his wife's sensitivities

(*Nesivos Olam, Nesiv Ahavas HaRei'a* 2). In the *tenaim* (articles of betrothal) it is stated explicitly that husband and wife "shall have joint control over their belongings." Depriving a wife of access to the family income is a frank violation of this condition.

From these *halachic* rulings is clear that the Torah does not give a husband the right to dominate the wife or to behave toward her in a way that offends her dignity, which is precisely what controlling her does.

Controlling another person is both futile and unethical. What then is meant by "he shall rule over you?" It can only mean that the husband is the *titular* head of the household. He sits at the head of the table and he recites the *kiddush* and the *hamotzi* blessing for the family. The husband occupies a titular but *not* a domineering position.

If we wish to know what the Torah requires of us, we should observe the behavior of our *tzaddikim*, who took great care to give their wives the respect that the Torah mandates.

To My Grandson

Although control problems may occur in any relationship, they are particularly dangerous in marriage. All of the desirable traits that contribute to a happy marriage can be undone by control.

A number of years ago, I wrote a rather lengthy letter to my grandson, with what I consider guidelines for a happy marriage. Although there may be some repetition of things already said, I prefer to present this letter *in toto* rather than edit it. Furthermore, some points deserve to be repeated.

■   ■   ■

My dear grandson:

Mazal tov on your engagement! Baruch Hashem, you have a lovely *kallah* and she comes from a beautiful family. You have been studying Torah diligently, and I know you to have fine *middos* (character traits). You should have a blissful marriage. May Hashem bless you both with the fulfillment of your hearts' desires.

My reason for writing this letter to you is that during my years of practice, I have often been consulted by couples who also could have been expected to have a blissful marriage, but unfortunately, things did not turn out that way. I have come to realize that even with the finest family backgrounds, and even where the young man and woman were excellent students in yeshivah and seminary respectively, there are many possible pitfalls in marriage.

Many things essential to a good marriage are well known. However, as Rabbi Moshe Chaim Luzzato says in *Path of the Just*, it is precisely those things that are familiar to us that we may take for granted and consequently not examine adequately. We know that being considerate is most important in a relationship. But just what does it mean to be considerate? It is possible for people to assume that they are considerate even though they may be lacking in this important trait.

I feel that many young men and women are simply not prepared well for the responsibilities of marriage and parenthood. Consequently, when stresses in these areas occur, they are at a loss how to deal with them properly, simply because they have never been taught the a b c's of human relationships.

Perhaps it was not all that essential for such guidance to be given in the past, but we are living in a different world today. In the environment in which we find ourselves, moral values have virtually disappeared, and hedonism has become the prevailing philosophy of life. The sanctity and strength of the traditional Jewish family has weakened. Attitudes totally alien to Yiddishkeit bombard us from all sides. The street is a toxic place, and some of the toxicity penetrates even our closed doors. We must have better preparation for marriage and family life.

The relationship of husband to wife is unlike any other relationship you have been in. It is different than that of child to parent or that of friend to friend. Children and parents, and friends to friends, are distinct from one another, regardless of how close they may feel. Of husband and wife, however, the Torah says, "They shall become one flesh" (*Genesis* 2:24). The Torah requires that a husband consider his wife as part of him. He should relate to her with the same care that he gives any other part of his person.

As you know, Torah observance requires more than following the *d'oraisa* (Scriptural ordinances). We must observe the Torah as interpreted by the Talmud, which says that "one should love one's wife as much as one loves oneself, and respect her even *more* than one respects oneself" (*Yevamos* 62b). The Talmud thus extends the consideration for one's wife beyond that of the Scripture. You have never experienced this type of relationship before. This is why I feel that guidance in this uniquely new relationship is essential.

This may be a good point to introduce several other passages in the Talmud that pertain to the husband/wife relationship. Remember, these are as binding upon us as any other *halachos*. Anyone who is meticulously observant of other *halachos* but is remiss in observance of the Talmudic teachings about the marriage relationship is derelict in Torah observance.

We would never think of a person who eats butter-fried chicken as being Torah observant. Neither should we consider a person who is derelict in following the Talmudic teaching of the husband/wife relationship as being Torah observant. It is unfortunate that some people place greater emphasis on ritual observance than on the quality of their relating to other people.

I must digress to emphasize this point. In Vilna, a shoemaker inherited great wealth, and achieved the local prominence often accorded to the wealthy. When he married off his daughter, there was an impressive procession from his home to the courtyard of the shul. One local citizen was upset by the shoemaker's rise to prominence. In the midst of the wedding procession he approached him with a pair of shoes. "Do you think you can have these repaired by tomorrow?" he asked.

R' Yisroel of Salant was appalled by this public humiliation. He said, "The previous rabbis of Vilna were called from *Gan Eden* to stand in judgement before the Heavenly Tribunal. They were being held responsible for not having sufficiently impressed upon the populace the importance of proper *middos*, which would have prevented the occurrence of a public humiliation."

The preservation of human dignity is of great importance, sometimes overriding a conflicting *halachah* (*Berachos* 19b). Think of it this way. A person who is very hungry is unable to control himself and goes into a McDonald's for a cheeseburger. He has committed a grave sin by frankly violating a Torah restriction, and he will be judged for this by the Heavenly Tribunal. However, this does not detract from the reward he may have earned by the study of Torah (*Sotah* 21a). On the other hand, a person who was diligently observant of Torah from childhood on, and at the age of eighty-four humiliates someone publicly and does not apologize, *loses reward for all the mitzvos he may have done throughout his entire lifetime* (*Ethics of the Fathers* 3:15). The Chafetz Chaim adds that this is true even if the humiliation occurs in private. That is the importance the Talmud gives to human dignity.

The dignity of one's spouse is no exception. There is no justification for disrespect of one's spouse.

Let us return now to some Talmudic statements.

"A person must always be cautious to respect his wife. The blessing in one's household is due *only* to the merit of one's wife, as the Torah says, 'He was good to Abraham because of her (Sarah)' " (*Genesis* 12:16, *Bava Metzia* 59a). We must weigh the Talmud's words carefully. We can hardly think of anything that could possibly surpass the spiritual greatness of the patriarch. Yet the Talmud says that the Divine blessings are by virtue *only* of the wife. Your study of Torah and observance of mitzvos, my dear grandson, are of inestimable value. But remember, the Divine *berachah* is by your wife's merits rather than yours.

"A person must be most cautious not to irritate his wife. Because she may be easily moved to tears, his punishment may be swift to come" (*Bava Metzia* 59a). The Talmud states that because a woman is exquisitely emotionally sensitive, great care must be taken to avoid upsetting her.

The Talmud relates that R' Rechumi was diligent in his Torah study in the academy of Rava, returning home Erev Yom Kippur. One time R' Rechumi was so deeply engrossed in Torah study that he was late in returning home. His wife awaited his return anxiously. "He is coming soon, he is coming soon," she said. When he did not come, she was distressed and dropped a tear from her eye. R' Rechumi was sitting on a roof at the time. The roof collapsed and he was killed (*Kesubos* 62b). So harsh a judgment for a single tear! And why was R' Rechumi late? Because he was studying Torah. Truly an amazing *gemara*.

Do not relate to your wife according to your own standards. You may be indifferent to things that may cause her distress. You may not give any significance to your birthday, and you might not care in the least whether or not she remembered it. But if your wife would feel slighted by your not remembering her birthday, you must make sure to remember it. Make note of days that may be important to her, especially her birthday and your anniversary.

It is irritating to me to hear the groundless aspersions that poorly informed people sometimes cast, saying that Torah favors men above women. They cite the fact that men have more mitzvos and are, therefore, more privileged. For years I have heard the *Kohanim* preface their *berachos* by saying that "G–d has sanctified us with the *kedushah* of Aaron." Not once have I felt inferior to *Kohanim* by my inability to pronounce the *berachos*, nor that I am not sanctified in the manner they are.

In sports, the team is supposed to do its utmost to win. Each player has a specific assignment. Can you imagine an outfielder protesting his position and insisting that he wants to be the catcher or vice versa? Players are assigned their positions by the judgment and decision of the manager. The outfielder and catcher are of equal importance to the team. Or think of a symphony orchestra in which the French horn player would say, "I want to play that melody. I don't want the violins to play it." Any individual player who puts his own career ahead of the team interest is a detriment to the team.

Our Manager has assigned roles to *Kohanim, Leviim* and Israelities, to women and to men. *Klal Yisrael* is a team. A woman who feels underprivileged fails to understand this. Men who consider themselves superior to women are equally in error.

There are some people who may be in error, and unfortunately, this misconception may sometimes be found even in people of authority. This is not a new phenomenon. The Talmud relates that when the daughters of Zelafchad heard that Eretz Yisrael was to be divided among the males, they took counsel and said, "G-d's compassion is not like that of humans. Humans are more considerate of males than of females. The Creator is not like that. His consideration is for both males and females, for it is written, 'He is good to all; His mercies are to all His works' " (*Sifri, Pinchas* 27).

We are commanded to emulate Hashem. "Just as He is merciful, so you should be merciful. Just as He is gracious, so you should be gracious" (*Shabbos* 133b). Anyone who lacks this impartiality is derelict in the commandment to emulate Hashem.

How thrilling it is to study Torah! There is little that can compare to the brilliance of the *Chidushei HaRim,* the clarity of the *Ketzos HaChoshen* or Reb Chaim's analysis and reconciliation of conflicting Rambam rulings. To whom do we owe all of this?

The Talmud says that the Jewish Torah world had become barren and that Torah would have been forgotten had it not been that the great R' Akiva restored it by teaching it to R' Meir, R' Shimon bar Yochai, R' Yosi ben Chalafta, R' Yehudah bar Elai and R' Nechemiah (*Yevamos* 62b). Torah was saved from extinction by R' Akiva, and we owe all our Torah knowledge to him.

As you know, R' Akiva was illiterate at age forty, and it was only at the behest of his wife, Rachel, that he went to study Torah. She sacrificed his company for twenty-five years so that he could excel in Torah. She cut off and sold her beautiful hair to support his learning. When he returned home with thousands of disciples, Rachel came to greet him. Not knowing who she was, R' Akiva's students blocked her access to the master. R' Akiva said to them, "Let her come. *Everything that I know in Torah and everything you know in Torah we owe to her*" (*Kesubos* 62-63). The next time you are enthralled with Torah, remember your obligation to Rachel.

As I watch the yeshivah students davening *Shemonah Esrei*, meditating and silently verbalizing the *tefillah*, I cannot but wonder whether they are aware that the most we know about *tefillah* is because of Hannah, the mother of the prophet Shmuel (*Berachos* 31b).

You are familiar with the Midrash that we merited liberation from the bondage of Egypt only by virtue of the righteous women (*Sotah* 11b). You also remember that not a single woman participated in the worship of the Golden Calf, a sin which cast its shadow over our entire painful history. And that when the spies returned with a negative report about the Promised Land, the lamentation of the Israelites caused a calamity from which we still suffer today. While the men demanded that Moses be deposed and a new leader appointed who will lead them back to the lime pits of Egypt, it was the women who insisted on proceeding to the conquest of Canaan (*Rashi, Numbers* 26:64).

When Jerusalem was destroyed and we were driven into exile, the Patriarchs Abraham, Isaac and Jacob pleaded to G–d for mercy for their children, but their pleas were not answered. Moses, whose supplication for Divine compassion was never turned away, was equally disregarded. It was only the intervention of the Matriarch Rachel that elicited the Divine response, "It is only by your merit, Rachel, that your children will be returned to their homeland" (Introduction to *Eichah Rabbah*).

Certainly you will wish your children to be Torah scholars. The groundwork for their success in Torah will be provided by your wife rather than you. Solomon says, "Hearken, my son, to the discipline of your father, and do not forsake *the Torah of your mother*" (*Proverbs* 1:8). It will be her emotional input in their infancy that will prepare them for your teaching. Indeed, at Sinai the instructions on receiving the Torah were given to the women before the men (*Rashi, Exodus* 19:4).

For everything precious to us — our liberation, our Torah knowledge, our *tefillah* and the ultimate Redemption — we are indebted to women. Little wonder that the Talmud accords the wife so lofty a status. It can only be crass ignorance that can cause a person's failure to appreciate the overriding role of the woman in Judaism.

But does the Torah not state that the man shall rule over his wife (*Genesis* 2:16)? It is evident from all our Torah ethical works that this "rule" means that the husband should be the *titular* head of the family. The husband sits at the head of the table, makes *kiddush* and recites the *hamotzi* for the family. This verse does not give a husband a right to be dictatorial or tyrannical.

Halachah requires that husband and wife respect one another. Rambam describes how the husband should respect the wife and how the wife should respect the husband (*Hilchos Ishus* 15:19-20). In your study of Rambam in the yeshivah you have been taught to pay close attention to every nuance in his great work. It is not only the content of the *halachah* that is important, but also just where he places the particular *halachah*. It is, therefore, noteworthy that Rambam placed the *halachah* of the husband's duty to respect his wife *before* that of the wife's respect for the husband. Of course, both are of equal importance and should be simultaneous. However, if anyone wished to make a case of where respect should begin, the Rambam's sequence provides the answer.

In the finest of relationships there are bound to be disagreements, but you must be careful how to disagree. The Torah decrees that a person must respect one's parents. If one sees his father committing a sin, one may not chastise him for it. *Halachah* states that one must say gently, "Father, is it not written in the Torah that this is not permissible?" *Halachah* teaches us how to disagree without being disrespectful.

Inasmuch as we have seen that the Talmud requires that a husband respect his wife even more than himself, disagreeing must be done respectfully. No shouting, no denouncing and certainly never using any derogatory or insulting terms.

Calm, gentle disagreement is not only necessary to fulfill one's duty to be respectful, but it is also wise and practical. When you raise your voice in an argument, your opponent becomes defensive. His attitude immediately changes from being receptive to what you are saying to thinking of how to counterattack. He tunes you out and may not even hear what you are saying. I have observed altercations in couples and have noted that they are often talking past each other. Neither has really heard what the other is saying.

If what you say has substance, say it quietly. You will make your point. Solomon says, "The gentle words of the wise are heard above the shouts of a ruler of fools" (*Ecclesiastes* 9:17). If you feel the need to shout, pause for a moment and rethink what you are about to say. Chances are you will find that your "argument is very weak."

Disagreements can be sensible discussions. They do not have to be arguments.

Many people have difficulty accepting constructive criticism. Solomon calls them fools and scoffers. "A scoffer does not like to be reproved; he will not go to the wise...A discerning heart looks for knowledge, but the mouth of fools feeds on non-wisdom" (*Proverbs* 15:12-14).

King Solomon says, "All of a person's ways appear right in his eyes" (ibid. 21:2). This is a psychological fact. We are generally oblivious of our own character defects. If others point them out to us, we may question their motives and doubt the validity of their criticism.

Hashem, in His infinite goodness, provided man with an *ezer kenegdo*, someone who can help him, but stand opposite him. A devoted wife is indeed one with her husband, yet she can stand aside and be more objective. Your wife may see things that you need to correct of which you may be unaware. Her bringing these to your attention is Hashem's special gift to you. A husband who reacts negatively to his wife's criticism is not only neglecting the opportunity to improve himself, but is also rejecting Hashem's kindness.

One of the reasons some young men do not know how to relate properly to a wife is because they had a paucity of modeling. Sometimes their parents did not provide the best examples. Many yeshivah boys look up to their Torah teachers and consciously or unconsciously emulate them. There is one important aspect of behavior that they do not observe. They have virtually no opportunity to see how their rebbe relates to his wife. Most of the accounts we have about the lives of our great Torah personalities were written by their students or *chassidim*. Very few children have been their parents' biographers. Children could have described how their parents related to each other. Unfortunately, there is a great void in this area.

In our generation we were privileged to have a Torah giant whose *middos* were exemplary. I suggest you obtain a biography of R' Shlomo Zalman Auerbach, a *gaon* and *tzaddik* whom I was privileged to know. There are many stories of how he ingeniously managed to respect the dignity of others even when there were *halachic* problems. He never transgressed *halachah*, but never embarrassed a person.

For example, R' Shlomo Zalman was on a bus (he felt that he had no right to take a taxi at the yeshivah's expense) when a scantly clad woman boarded and sat next to him. He waited a few moments, then rang the bell and smilingly said to her, "Pardon me, but I must get off here." He got off and waited for the next bus. Someone who had observed him asked why he had done this. R' Shlomo Zalman replied, "What else could I do? I could not continue to sit there. If I had moved to another seat that would have insulted her. Just because she does not dress with *tznius* does not give me the right to insult her." R' Shlomo Zalman was a *gadol* in *middos* as well as in *halachah*.

When R' Shlomo Zalman's wife died, he said, "It is customary to ask *mechilah* (pardon) from the departed person for any offense one might have committed toward them. We lived our lives according to the Torah, so there is really nothing for which I must ask *mechilah*. Nevertheless, since it is a *minhag*, I will comply with it."

Can you imagine this? A person who lived with another person in a close relationship for some sixty years and is secure in the knowledge that he never offended her, even once in sixty years? This would be difficult to believe of anyone except for R' Shlomo Zalman.

"We lived our lives according to Torah," and that is why there was no need to ask *mechilah*. This was not the aspects of Torah that deal with Shabbos or *kashrus*. This was the aspect of Torah that deals with proper behavior between man and wife. There are many people who may truthfully state, "I never ate *tereifah* all my life" or "I never missed a single day of putting on *tefillin*." How many people can truthfully say that during many years of marriage they never offended their wife? To R' Shlomo Zalman, the Torah guidelines for proper behavior toward a wife were of no less importance than the laws of Shabbos and *kashrus*. This is what it means to lead a Torah-true life.

A woman once complained to R' Aryeh Levin that her husband acted abusively toward her, and would he please speak to him about this. R' Aryeh told her that if he would chastise him, he might become even more abusive toward her for having "tattled" on him. "I will have an opportunity to speak about this without revealing that you have spoken to me," he said.

R' Aryeh would teach *Ein Yaakov* between *minchah* and *maariv*, and this man regularly attended these sessions. When he came to a portion that discussed relationships, R' Aryeh elaborated emphatically and at great length on the Torah requirements for respecting one's wife, and how harsh the Divine punishment is for causing her distress.

R' Aryeh's teacher and mentor, the great *gaon* and *tzaddik* R' Issar Zalman Melzer, happened to be in the shul at the time. He said to R' Aryeh, "I must express my gratitude for your lecture today. I have not thought enough about whether I am observing the Torah requirements for respecting my wife properly. Your lecture has reminded me that I must do some soul-searching."

Why is it that those people who need it the least hear it the most?

You should realize that although your wife loves you very much, you are nevertheless a newcomer in her life. For the past two decades her relationships have been with her parents, siblings and extended family. These relationships are very dear to her and you should respect them.

As a Torah scholar you remember that the Torah says, "Therefore a man shall leave his father and mother and cleave unto his wife" (*Genesis* 2:24). Note that it does not say the reverse. Apparently it is easier for a man to detach from his family than for a woman.

Some men, probably because of feelings of inferiority, may misinterpret the wife's desire to be with her family as a reflection of her love for him. "If she really loved me why would she still need to be with her family so often?" It is foolish to make an unreasonable demand for the wife to have no other needs in the world except for the relationship with her husband. I have seen egocrazed husbands who demanded virtual worship from their wives.

There are some accepted customs, such as, with whom does the young couple spend the first Seder? Regardless of what the custom is, be sensitive to your wife's needs. Remember, the Talmud says that her emotional needs are greater than yours.

Never, but never belittle your wife's family. Remember, she loved and respected them long before she loved and respected you. If you think you are going to gain in stature by belittling them, you could not possibly be more wrong. The Talmud says that an honorable person is one who *gives* respect, rather than one who receives honors (*Ethics of the Fathers* 4:1).

The idea that "things must be done my way" has ruined many marriages.

Zeide was very dedicated to his heritage. Nevertheless, he sang *Shalom Aleichem* the way Bobbe's father did rather than how his father did. He also adopted a number of other practices of Bobbe's father. This was not only to assuage her homesickness, but also to indicate that he valued her family's *minhagim*. This is just a tiny example of Zeide's sensitivity and consideration for Bobbe.

This relationship is very new to you. Keep that in mind. There are many things you will learn as you go along. As long as you are sensitive and considerate, you will integrate this new knowledge.

I have every reason to believe that your marriage will be blissful. You and your *kallah* have found each other by the tried and true method that has been in our family and culture for many centuries. However, the rationale for this method must be understood so that it can result in a happy marriage.

In Western civilization, marriages are based on what is referred to as "love." A young man and young woman "fall in love" and decide to marry. The fact that the incidence of failed marriages is so high in this culture should raise some eyebrows. Where is the flaw in this method?

The Rebbe of Kotzk once saw a young man obviously enjoying a dish of fish. "Why are you eating the fish?" the Rebbe asked.

The young man looked puzzled. "Why? Because I love fish," he said.

"Oh," the Rebbe said, "and it was because of your love for the fish that you took it out of the water, killed it and cooked it. That is a strange way to show your love.

"The reason you did that, young man," the Rebbe continued, "is not because you love the fish. What you love is *yourself*. Because of your self-love, you wish to satisfy your appetite. The fish tastes good to you, so you killed it for your own gratification. There is nothing wrong with that. Just do not delude yourself that you love the fish."

The Rebbe of Kotzk made an excellent point. Much of what Western civilization calls "love" is not really the love of another person, but rather self-love, "fish-love," if you will.

A young man and a young woman meet. He feels that she can provide for all his emotional needs, and she feels that he can provide for her emotional needs. This is called "falling in love." There is indeed a love relationship, but it is essentially a self-love.

A marriage based on self-love is on unsure grounds. Suppose that after some time the man thinks that there is another woman who can better provide for his emotional needs. If self-love is the cement of the relationship, it stands to reason that he may wish to terminate the first relationship. Also, infatuation may blind the young people to major differences in their outlook on life. When this phase passes, incompatibilities may come to the surface.

The advantage of a *shidduch* is that both partners usually come from similar backgrounds, and this may eliminate areas of ideological conflict. Limited contact prior to the engagement reduces the possible distortion of judgment due to infatuation. However, even in the best of situations it is still possible that the young man or young woman or both enter the marriage with their own agenda. Self-interest may still be a dominant factor, and frustration of gratifying the self-interest may cause difficulties in the relationship.

Couples who seek marriage counseling are often told that their problem is one of communication. They are not communicating well to each other. That may be true, but I suspect that the cause is not always faulty communication.

One time at the airport I was standing near a man on the moving walkway. He recognized someone on the adjacent moving walkway going in the opposite direction. They exchanged a few words, but were soon out of range of communication. These people may both have had excellent skills in communication. The reason their communication failed was because they were heading in opposite directions.

If a young man is primarily interested that the marriage relationship should provide for *his* needs, and the young woman is interested that the marriage provide fulfillment of *her* needs, the two may be heading in different directions. There is no common goal that sets them on the same path.

At the wedding ceremony, the first *berachah* after the giving of the ring is *shehakol bara lichvodo*, that Hashem created everything for His glory. This is indeed a wonderful concept, but what is its relevance to marriage?

I believe that the Sages instituted this *berachah* to tell the young couple that they should have a common goal. Their primary function should be to establish a family that will bring honor to the Name of Hashem. The Talmud gives us the formula for this. "If a person transacts business honestly and behaves respectfully, people will say, 'How fortunate are the parents who bore him, and how fortunate is the teacher who taught him Torah' " (*Yoma* 86a). Establishing a family that manifests the high ethics of Torah is a *kiddush Hashem*. That is the couple's foremost responsibility and this should constitute the principal reason for marriage.

There is no denying that both husband and wife should have their emotional needs met. However, if these are the primary basis for the marriage and they are frustrated, the relationship may falter. If the prime purpose is *shehakol bara lichvodo*, there is a firm basis for the relationship that can enable it to sail through stormy seas.

A healthy marriage can exist only when there is mutual trust between husband and wife. Concealing or withholding important information can be ruinous to the relationship. Of course, information that was given to either one in confidence cannot be revealed, and both partners should understand why they must respect a person's confidence. Keeping this kind of a secret to yourself is not detrimental. However, withholding information that the other spouse has every right to know undermines the trust that is so vital in a marriage.

Of course, the rules of *lashon hara* must be observed. A husband or wife may hear a juicy piece of gossip and just can't wait to get home to tell it to the spouse. The restrictions against *lashon hara* apply within the family as well. If the husband hears about something and then discovers that his wife knew about it three weeks ago, he may say, "Why didn't you tell me?" She should reply, "Because it's *lashon hara*, Honey. Remember?"

One of the problems I run into with some frequency is a parent who calls, "My son/daughter is 20. Two years ago he/she was treated for depression, obsessive-compulsive disorder or panic disorder. He/she is fine now. We are involved in *shidduchim* now. Am I obliged to reveal this? If I do, it may ruin the chance of a *shidduch*."

I not only empathize with the parents, but I agonize with them. I do not believe one must tell the *shadchan*, and it is not necessary to reveal this at the first meeting. However, if it seems that the *shidduch* may progress, I firmly believe that the party must say, "There is something I must share with you. I had this problem for which I was treated." If the person is still taking medication, this must be revealed. It is unthinkable to enter a relationship as intimate as marriage with deception. Every *posek* I have consulted has said that it is obligatory to reveal such information.

Poskim have told me that the Chafetz Chaim, the greatest authority on *lashon hara*, says that if someone knows that a party to a pending *shidduch* had a condition, which, if known to the other side, would discourage them from the *shidduch, one is obligated to reveal such information even if not asked!* Failure to do so violates *lo taamod al dam re'acha,* "Do not stand by while your fellow's blood is being shed."

The parents are understandably reluctant to reveal something which would prevent the success of the *shidduch*. I ask them, "How would you feel if the situation were reversed? What would you say if after your son/daughter was married, it was discovered that important information was withheld?" Even though they realize that they would feel deceived, they still may not be able to get themselves to reveal the information.

I know of several cases where the information was withheld, only to be discovered after the marriage. It has always been disastrous to the marriage.

The sum total of this is that a husband and wife must have complete trust in each other. Trust is the single most important component of a successful marriage. *Never do anything that might jeopardize your wife's trust in you.*

Let me change the subject. You have never had a wife before. You have no idea of what any wife expects, and you do not know what your wife will expect of you. She may be upset because you did not ask her whether she needs a new dress for her cousin's upcoming wedding. She may point out that her father always would ask her mother whether she needed a new dress for a wedding. Of course, when she remembers her father's asking this, her parents had already been married for a number of years. Her father probably did not know to do this three months after their marriage either. You might say, "Honey, I'm not good at guessing. Eventually I will learn, but please, when you want something, tell me. It's the only way I can know."

Speaking of a dress, let me mention what the *Menoras Hamaor* says (Ner 3): "Economize on your own clothes. Clothe your children according to your means, but extend yourself beyond your means for your wife's clothes."

You should realize that women are physiologically different then men. They have hormonal changes that men do not have. Some women may experience moods due to these hormonal changes. They may be irritable, angry or may cry for no apparent reason. After a few days this disappears and they are as pleasant and jolly as ever. If this is not understood, a husband may be bewildered and the wife may be desperate. They may each think something is wrong mentally. Each may blame themselves or the other partner.

Such mood changes are not uncommon and can be managed fairly easily if properly understood. I believe that in preparation for marriage it would help if you read my book *Getting Up When You're Down*; it can eliminate unnecessary aggravation.

You should know that your wife is your wife and that she is not your mother. She does not have to be like your mother. Your mother may have catered to you because she raised you from infancy. Don't expect this of your wife.

You may have different tastes in foods. You may love gefilte fish and she cannot stand it. At her home they began the Shabbos morning meal with chopped liver, while you are accustomed to fish in the morning. I trust that you are far too intelligent to make an issue of such trivia.

Your mother may have been a meticulous housekeeper. "You could eat off the floor." Your wife's mother may not have observed that standard.

One newlywed young man complained to his rosh yeshivah that his wife was not a good *balebosta* (housekeeper). The following day he answered the door and was surprised to see his esteemed rosh yeshivah, who came into the house, found the broom, dust-pan and mop, and showed the young man how to clean up.

By the way, there is a tradition that one should do something to help prepare for Shabbos. That is in addition to mopping the floor.

A young man consulted the Steipler Gaon about a difficult *gemara*. As the young man was about to leave, the Steipler said, "Young man, I see that you are a *masmid* (diligent student). Don't forget to help your wife at home."

The young man said, "My wife is a true *eishes chail* (woman of valor). Her greatest wish is that I learn Torah."

The Steipler nodded. "Yes," he said, "that is *her* mitzvah. *Your* mitzvah is to help at home."

Hashem will bless you with children. Infants get up several times during the night to be nursed or fed. You enjoy your sleep and hate being awoken. Furthermore, you cannot nurse the baby, so what point is there in your getting up?

Pregnancy and childbirth are indeed normal conditions, but they are a drain on a woman's energy. After childbirth, a mother needs much rest. (Another reason why you should read *Getting Up When You're Down.*) When you hear the baby cry, get up, diaper the baby and give him/her to your wife. When the feeding is over, the baby needs to be burped. Let your wife go back to sleep. You burp the baby.

"But," you may say, "I need my sleep. If I get up to the baby I will not be able to concentrate well on my learning tomorrow." I suspect that this is the rationalization of the *yetzer hara* rather than the counsel of the *yetzer tov*.

You can become a *gaon* from burping the baby! Your uncles were born when I was in medical school. During the night, I would put a medical text on the dresser and read while I burped the baby. This was an excellent time for study, and I am certain this enabled me to graduate with honors! Don't lose this opportunity. Place a *sefer* on the dresser. You will learn much and have a healthy, well-rested wife.

The Alter Rebbe's living quarters were above those of his son, the Mittler Rebbe. One time the Alter Rebbe heard an infant crying incessantly. He went down and found the Mittler Rebbe so engrossed in Torah study that he did not hear the baby's cry. The Alter Rebbe sharply rebuked his son. As great as Torah study is, it should never make one oblivious to a child's cry.

Your in-laws will come to visit. *Halachah* requires that you respect them. Incidentally, there are a lot of jokes about mothers-in-law. Don't tell them to your wife. This is not cute. You would not want to hear such comments about your mother.

One of the vexing problems today is whether a woman should work, pursue a career or be a homemaker. Western civilization has been influenced by the feminist movement. There are many things about this movement that are valid. For example, there is no reason why a woman should be paid less than a man for the selfsame job. But there are other things that are not as clear.

There is no denying that until recently our society has been male dominated. Some women have rebelled against this, and there have indeed been some changes. In my medical school class there were 98 men and 4 women. Today half or more of a medical school or law school class may be women. There is a misconceived attitude that unless a woman has a professional or business career, she is admitting her inferiority to men.

You can't build walls against attitudes. Some young women who were taught Torah *hashkofos* (outlooks) in seminary may nevertheless envy the woman who has become a lawyer or CEO of a major firm. Furthermore, it is possible that even some men secretly admire a woman who has made such an achievement. The woman who has five children, three of them in diapers, may have a feeling of missing out on success in life, and possibly even of oppression. She may feel she has little to show for herself if at the end of the day she is totally exhausted and is confronted by a huge pile of laundry and a table full of dirty dishes.

Granted, it is often necessary for a wife to work. It is also a common practice that the wife may be helping support the husband who is learning in *kollel*. She may be happy to do so, because she was taught that this is her *tafkid* (purpose). She gladly works and does her utmost to care for the children and the household. All this notwithstanding, she is only human, and is subject to viewing with some envy the professional woman whose life seems to be so much more glamorous and less stressful.

Rabbi Akiva gave his wife, Rachel, a gold necklace and pendant of Jerusalem. He said, "She certainly deserves this. She sacrificed so much for Torah." You must take every opportunity to acknowledge your appreciation of your wife's efforts. Showing how you value her can help offset the cultural glorification of the career woman.

In addition to the respect which is her due, your children will learn from you to respect their mother. Just as parents have an obligation to give proper *chinuch* (training) to their children in all other mitzvos, they are equally obligated to give them *chinuch* in respect for their parents. This is not accomplished by lecturing, but by modeling. They will respect their mother if you do.

You may enjoy teasing. There is a proverb, "*Wer es liebt sich, necht sich*" (People who love each other tease each other). My advice to you: *Don't tease!* There are much better ways of expressing affection. What you may think is clever and cute might be felt by your wife as a sharp sting. Stinging remarks are not easily forgotten.

There are some men who are domineering and give orders to their wives as though they were five-star generals. They justify their behavior by quoting the statement that is indeed cited in *halachah*, "A proper woman is one who does the will of her husband."

Our Sages are very critical of people who distort Torah for their own needs. What if the husband wanted her to cook something for him on Shabbos? Is she to do his will in order to be a "proper wife?" In order to understand what this statement means, we must know its origin.

The Scripture gives of an account of a battle between the armies of Sisera and Israel. Sisera's forces were defeated and he fled, finding asylum in the tent of Yael, a Kenite woman. Yael knew that her husband had a peace agreement with Sisera. However, realizing that

Sisera was a threat to Israel, she knew that her husband valued Israel above Sisera. When Sisera fell asleep in her tent, she killed him. She had correctly interpreted her husband's will. The Sages, therefore, cite her as an example of a woman who understands what her husband would want her to do under certain circumstances.

How one can distort this to give a husband dictatorial rights is beyond me. There is no justification for tyrannical behavior.

I observed my parents' marriage for forty-three years. There was profound mutual respect, consideration and love. As you know, Zeide first met Bobbe *after* the *chuppah*. Their marriage was not based on "fish-love." The stresses they went through early in their marriage would have destroyed a "fish-love" relationship. The only complaint I remember Bobbe having is that after fifty years of married life she still did not know what foods Zeide preferred. He ate whatever she prepared. To have shown a preference would have meant that she might have to go out of her way or do something extra. Conserving Bobbe's energy was far more important to him than what food he enjoyed.

You know that when Zeide found out that he had pancreatic cancer, he took it right in stride. Zeide knew a great deal about medicine, and was correct in his assessment that chemotherapy for this type of cancer was not effective. He said to me, "If it could prolong my life, I would have to accept the unpleasant side effects. But to suffer for no purpose makes no sense." I agreed that there was no point in chemotherapy.

The doctor who spoke to Bobbe told her that the most that could be expected from chemotherapy was another three months. Bobbe said, "Three months? Why, to extend his life for even three days you would have to do it."

Zeide said to me, "I'm sorry the doctor gave Bobbe false hope. But if I do not take the chemotherapy, then when I die, Bobbe will say, 'Why didn't I insist on it? He might still be alive!' Bobbe will then feel guilty, and I wouldn't want that. So I will take the chemotherapy with all its miseries. I've done many things for Bobbe. This gives me a chance to do the last thing I can for her."

This was not "fish-love."

There is a natural tendency to blame things on others. That is how mankind got into trouble right at the beginning. When G–d asked Adam if he had eaten from the forbidden fruit, his response was, "My wife made me do it." Eve, in turn, blamed the serpent. Neither accepted responsibility for their actions. Perhaps if Adam had said, "I did wrong and I regret it," he would have been forgiven and the course of world history might have been much different.

Rashi points out how strong the urge to divest oneself of responsibility can be. The Matriarch Rachel was desperate to have children. So much so that she said, "If I have no children I might as well die" (*Genesis* 30:10). The Midrash says that when Joseph was born and her fondest wish was realized, she said, "Now if something breaks I will have someone to blame it on. I can say that the baby did it" (ibid. 30:23, *Rashi*). Think of it! Is it imaginable that in her moment of supreme joy, when she felt that she finally had something to live for, our mother Rachel was happy because she will now have someone to blame for a dish being broken? It is clear that the Midrash tells us this only to impress upon us the intensity of the urge to place blame on someone else.

The reason the Torah tells this about Adam and Rachel is to alert us about the proclivity of people to blame others. Be very careful of this human frailty.

Why is this tendency to blame others so strong? Because if we can blame others then we do not feel we have to make any changes in ourselves. "It's the other people's fault. Let them change. I'm fine the way I am."

We are creatures of habit. We are set in our ways and we do not like to change. Blaming others allows us to stay the way we are. This is as natural a response as reflexively putting your hand in front of your face to protect yourself from a flying object. You must catch yourself and make a concerted effort to avoid blaming. But I can assure you that if you succeed in refraining from blaming, it will be a major contribution to a happy marriage.

The Talmud says that when a man and woman are united in marriage, Hashem makes His presence dwell with them (*Sotah* 17a). That is, if you let Him.

When the Rebbe of Kotzk was a young man, R' Bunim of P'shische asked him, "Young man, where is G-d?"

"There is no place where He is not present," the young R' Mendel answered.

"Young man, I asked you, 'Where is G-d?' " R' Bunim repeated.

"The whole world is full of His glory," R' Mendel answered.

Again R' Bunim said, "Young man, I have asked you, 'Where is G-d?' "

R' Mendel said, "If my answers do not satisfy you, then you tell me."

R' Bunim said, "G-d is present wherever He is invited to be."

Yes, G-d is everywhere, but we can cause Him to withdraw His presence.

There are essentially two human traits that repel Hashem. One is *gaavah* (vanity). Hashem says, "I cannot be in the presence of a vain person." Earlier I pointed out the grievous error of men considering women to be inferior. If a husband has an attitude of superiority, which is generally manifested by his being demanding, domineering and inconsiderate of his wife, he drives Hashem away. My dear grandson, I regret to tell you that I know of homes where all the mitzvos are meticulously observed, but it is a home devoid of Hashem's presence because someone there is a *baal gaavah*.

The other thing that repels Hashem is idolatry. Of course, there will never be any idols in your home. That is just unthinkable. Statue idols, that is. But if you fly into a rage, that is equivalent to idolatry (*Rambam, Hilchos Daius* 2). I can understand that you may feel angry when provoked, but you must exercise great restraint not to erupt into a rage. If you lose your temper, it is equivalent to removing all the *mezuzos* from your doors. Hashem does not want to be in a place where there is idol worship. That is precisely what happens when a person loses control of his anger.

Earlier I quoted the Torah's description of the marriage relationship, "They shall be as one flesh." Husband and wife should be one. Now if you injured your foot, would you become angry at it for causing you pain? Would you hit your foot? A Torah observing person fulfills the Torah concept of marriage. It should be as absurd to be angry at your wife as at any other part of you. You may feel hurt, but not angry.

You may say, "Zeide, what is it that you are expecting of me? I am not an angel!"

Some people think that it is beyond human capacity to observe Shabbos appropriately, or to avoid any foods that may contain a trace of something non-kosher. They may say, "How can you expect me to make a living if I refuse to work on Shabbos? Or, it is the only time I can visit my friends, do my chores or make necessary contacts. I cannot possibly avoid traveling or using the telephone." Or someone may say, "My work requires me to travel all over the country all week. I cannot possibly adhere to strict *kashrus*. What do you want me to do, starve? I am a human being, not an angel."

It is only a matter of degree. One does not have to be an angel to observe Shabbos and *kashrus*, and one does not have to be an angel to control one's temper. Nor does one have to be an angel to think of his wife as part of him and act accordingly. Zeide was not an angel. He was a great person, a superb human being. And by the way, that is better than being an angel.

Although achieving control over anger may be difficult, you can get a great assist from the letter of the Ramban to his son. Not only does it contain excellent instructions, but the Ramban also says that on the day one reads it, his prayers will be answered. Of course, the Ramban is not referring to prayers for winning the lottery, but to prayers for greater spirituality. Ramban suggests you read this letter once a week. I recommend that you make a fixed time each week for reading this letter.

The Talmud is very harsh with husbands who terrorize their household. "Whoever exercises excessive fear over his household will eventually come to transgress the three sins: forbidden relations, bloodshed and violation of Shabbos" (*Gittin* 6b). If Shabbos preparations are lagging late on Friday afternoon, the instructions to get things ready must be said in a soft, pleasant tone (*Shabbos* 34a).

Rabbi Zeira lived to an old age. When his students asked by what merit he achieved his longevity, he said, "I never raised my voice in my house" (*Megillah* 28a). Speaking gently contributes to everyone's longevity.

While there is some controversy about what portions of Torah women should study, there is universal agreement that they should learn about the mitzvos incumbent upon them. This includes not only the laws of Shabbos but also the mitzvah of *emunah* (belief) and all the *middos* required by Torah. I suggest that you have a *shiur* with your wife in *seforim* such as *Mesilas Yeshorim* and *Chovas Halevovos*. Learning Torah together creates a strong bond.

I suggest that you and your wife begin to prepare yourself for being parents by reading books on parenting. We don't come into the world as accomplished doctors, lawyers or electricians. Much study is necessary to acquire these skills. There is no reason to assume that we are natural born competent parents.

Unless there is adequate preparation for parenting, parents may have divergent ideas about raising children. This can cause much confusion for the child. The time to decide on a course that both parents agree on is *before* the children are born.

The commentaries on *tefillah* ask, Why is it necessary to verbalize our prayers? Inasmuch as Hashem knows our innermost thoughts, why do we simply not meditate? What is gained by pronouncing the words?

Various answers have been given. I am bold enough to suggest an additional answer.

There appears to be an inner resistance to acknowledging gratitude. Already the first human being, Adam, was an ingrate (*Rashi, Genesis* 3:12). Moses sharply rebuked the Israelites for being ingrates. This reluctance can be seen even in small children. Mother may say, "Now say 'thank you' to the nice man for the candy," and the child replies with a grunt that indicates that he has no intention of doing so.

Tosafos (*Avodah Zarah* 5a) says that the reason the Israelites did not want to acknowledge their gratitude to Hashem was because they did not want to feel beholden to Him. This is a profound psychological insight. When we have strong negative feelings about something, our minds may render us oblivious to it. Even small children may react this way.

It is even more difficult to feel obligated and beholden to another human being than it is to Hashem. We may find it easier to express our gratitude to Hashem. If we do so frequently, and accustom ourselves to pronounce the words "I thank you" to Hashem, we may lower the resistance to saying them to another person. This is one advantage of verbalizing our prayers.

A second area where there is some resistance is the expression of love for another person. During courtship, a young man and a young woman may indeed say "I love you" or write these words on the card accompanying a gift or flowers. For some strange reason, marriage seems to curtail the expression of love. A couple may live together for fifty years without verbally expressing their love for each other. Each may say, "Why do I have to say it? He/she knows I love him/her." True, but it is still very pleasant and reassuring to hear it.

When we declare our love to Hashem in prayer, we realize that although we love Hashem and Hashem knows we love Him, we express it verbally anyway. That is a good precedent. We should apply it to the people we love.

In *tefillah* we confess our sins. We express our regret for having done wrong and pledge not to repeat our sins. In human interaction, admitting one was wrong is met with great resistance. People may rationalize and justify their actions and may be obstinate in refusing to admit they were wrong. When we say to Hashem, "I have sinned and I ask Your forgiveness," we may reduce the resistance to saying this to other people.

My dear grandson, if there is any formula for a successful marriage, it is to utilize these expressions when they are called for. The three short phrases, "I thank you," "I love you" and "I am sorry for what I did. I was wrong," are a magic charm for making the marriage a happy one.

As was noted earlier, true love for another person is an unselfish love. There is a beautiful chassidic story that illustrates this.

The *tzaddik,* R' Moshe Leib of Sassov, has come down in chassidic lore as outstanding in *ahavas Yisrael.* R' Moshe Leib said that he learned what *ahavah* means from a drunkard.

While passing a tavern, R' Moshe Leib overheard a conversation between two inebriated men. "I love you, Stepan," the first one said.

"You just say that, Ivan," Stepan responded. "You don't really love me." The two kept on exchanging these assertions until Stepan finally said, "If you really love me, Ivan, then tell me, where am I hurting?"

R' Moshe Leib said, "*Ahavas Yisrael* means to know other people's pain without them telling you so."

This is the kind of love that should develop between husband and wife. Just as one knows one's own needs, wants and pains, so one should know that of the spouse. I don't expect this to occur at the very beginning of the relationship. However, it will develop if you make a concerted effort to develop it.

My dear grandson, be extremely cautious about your words. I think that the reason our Sages formulate the prayer "*Boruch Sheamar vehaya olam,* Blessed is He Who spoke and the world came into being" instead of "*Boruch Borei Haolam,* Blessed is the Creator of the world," is because they wished to stress that the spoken word can create an entire world. By the same token, a spoken word can destroy a world. The prophet says "Their tongue is like a sharp arrow" (*Jeremiah* 9:7). Actually, the tongue is even more powerful than an arrow. A suit of armor can repel an arrow. Sharp words can pierce the strongest armor. Some of the wisest words spoken by a human being are those in the letter of the Ramban: "Think about what you wish to say before you say it." I cannot begin to tell you how much misery would have been avoided if people would have followed the Ramban's advice.

In the best of relationships unforeseen problems may arise. It is extremely important to nip these in the bud. Unresolved problems tend to linger and not go away. To the contrary, they may become more complicated with time.

It is indeed important to have a *chaver* in whom you can confide. However, if any problem arises in the relationship, *physical or emotional,* do not ask your peers for advice. Seek the advice of wisdom and experience.

You will remember that when Solomon died and Rehavam inherited the throne, he was confronted by the populace that wanted the taxation to be eased. The elders counseled Rehavam to be flexible and respect the complaints of the populace. Rehavam's peers advised him to take a hard line and assert his authority. Rehavam favored the advice of his peers over the counsel of his elders, precipitating a catastrophic partition of Israel from which we have never recovered.

Choose an older person who is wise with experience. Of course, age in itself is no guarantee of wisdom, but you can certainly find a person whose maturity and clarity of thought make him a resource for advice. If necessary, do not hesitate to seek the advice of a professional counselor.

I can testify that, as a psychiatrist, I have been consulted by people with serious marital problems. In many instances these problems could have been avoided had they been dealt with at the onset, when their resolution was relatively simple. The couple did not seek professional help earlier either because they felt they could work it out themselves or, more often, because they felt embarrassed to do so. There is still a widespread attitude that there is a stigma to consulting a professional counselor, and people may look for help only when the problem has reached desperate proportions. Do not be so foolish.

People who detect a minor problem with their automobile are likely to consult a mechanic promptly. They generally do not consult their friends, and they certainly do not wait until the car breaks down before asking for competent help.

We are not born mechanics or doctors. It takes study and experience to develop these skills. Neither are we born as competent spouses or parents. Being a spouse or parent is a huge responsibility, and we should realize that we need education and training to achieve competence.

Which brings me to the next item. One of the great mysteries is why Hashem arranged it so that people have their greatest wisdom when they need it least. By the time a person reaches retirement age, life has taught him a great deal. However, at this point he does not have to make any major decisions. The really important decisions — whom to marry, what kind of a career to choose, where to live, how to raise one's children — these are all made when we are young and inexperienced. Why do we not have our maximum wisdom between ages eighteen and thirty, when we needed it most?

I can only conclude that in His infinite wisdom, Hashem knows that maximum energy and maximum wisdom do not go together. When we are young, we have maximum energy, but our wisdom is at its lowest. When we are old, we have our maximum wisdom, but our energy is at its lowest.

What is the solution? It is that energetic youth should avail themselves of the wisdom of the elders. That is the best of all possible worlds. Unfortunately, many young people are headstrong and think they know it all. This can result in tragic consequences. So be wise, and apply your great energies guided by the wisdom of experience.

One of the first things you and your wife should do is to read authentic books on parenting and discuss the various issues. You may choose *Positive Parenting* as a starter. This was written with the collaboration of one of the finest child psychologists in the country. This will give you and your wife an opportunity to have a unified and consistent approach in parenting.

Young children are exceedingly shrewd. They know how to play one parent against the other. Proper preparation can help you avoid this.

I know that I made some mistakes in raising my children, and your parents no doubt made their mistakes. You are entitled to make mistakes, but do not repeat our mistakes. These are avoidable.

Children need both love and discipline. These two may sometimes appear to be in conflict, but with proper education, discipline can be seen as love. However, it must be discipline that is directed toward the child's betterment rather than a result of parents' anger or frustration. Uneducated parents may vacillate between lenience and firmness. There is nothing as confusing to a child as the inconsistency of their parents.

Preparing yourselves before the children come onto the scene is most advantageous. An ounce of prevention is worth a ton of cure. Once problems arise, you are in a state of stress and this may result in knee-jerk reactions. Discussing in advance how you will raise your children can prevent many problems.

My dear grandson, you will be bringing children into this world. Your relationship to your children will derive from an inborn love of a parent for a child. There was no need for the Torah to tell parents to care for their children. The Torah does, however, instruct children to respect and revere their parents. This is not inborn trait.

That is the way the history of mankind began. Adam and Eve cared for their children. They had no parents to care for. This is the way it has continued through history.

Children do not ask to be brought into this difficult world. It is the parent's decision. Parents, therefore, have an obligation to provide their children with the best means to adjust to this world. Their motivation should be to do what is best for their children. The children should not be used primarily as a means of fulfilling the parents' needs.

I see two-year-old children running around dressed in designer clothes. Two-year-olds have no concept about designer clothes. They can be just as warm in less expensive clothes. It is the parents' ego to show others that they are buying designer clothes for their children. This may seem to be trivial, but it indicates that parents may exploit their children for their own ego. This can sometimes have serious consequences. Children should feel that the parents have *their* interest at heart.

Your children will respect and honor you as the Torah commands. It is important, however, that they know that you consider yourself valuable to them as a parent. Some parents spend so much time at work that they do not have much time to spend with their children. They may say, "I have to spend this time at work so that I can provide the children with all their needs."

Yes, children indeed have many needs that require money. However, they also have a great need for closeness with their parents. Giving them *things* instead of *yourself* is making a statement that you consider the things you give them as being of greater value than yourself. If parents so degrade themselves, it is little wonder that the children's respect for them may suffer.

Self-respect, respect for others and being respected by others go hand-in-hand. If you give of yourself to your children, you are making a statement that you have self-respect, and this encourages them to respect you.

I mentioned the fact that the Rambam places the duties of the husband toward his wife before those of the husband, and that this should teach us who must initiate respect for the other. There is another nuance in this Rambam that is often overlooked.

Rambam says that "a husband should respect his wife more than himself and love her as he loves himself" (*Hilchos Ishus* 15:19). The origin of this *halachah* is the Talmud cited earlier, that "one should love one's wife as much as one loves oneself, and respect her *even more* than one respects oneself" (*Yevamos* 62b). Why does Rambam reverse the order of the Talmud, placing respect *before* love?

I think the reason is that to love one's wife as much as one loves oneself cannot be achieved from the first moment of marriage. A strong love develops gradually. However, *respect can begin from the very first moment.*

I am sure that by following these teachings of Rambam and by developing your *middos* according to the works of *chassidus* and *mussar,* your marriage will indeed be one of enduring happiness.

Like Adam and Eve in *Gan Eden*

At a wedding, a rabbi remarked on the *berachah* (blessing) that G–d should bless the new couple with the joy of Adam and Eve in *Gan Eden*, "That means that they should be free of meddling parents and in-law trouble just like Adam and Eve in *Gan Eden*."

Many young couples encounter difficulties from parents and parents-in-law whom they see as "meddling." Some choose to ignore the problem and make believe it does not exist. No problem is ever resolved by "make believe." However, in order to address the problem constructively, some understanding is required. Understanding does *not* mean approving or justifying.

Understanding enables one to have an attitude that is more conducive to solving a problem.

Understanding is what my mother used to refer to as "the holy al tadin." She was referring to the statement al tadin es chavercha ad shetagia limkomo, "Do not judge a person until you have put yourself in his place" (Ethics of the Fathers 2:5). She referred to this statement as "holy" because it is the key to resolving problems across a broad spectrum of relationships. In psychology we refer to this as empathy, which means seeing a situation from another person's perspective. Granted, that perspective may be distorted, but one must be able to understand that to that person, his perspective is reality. Someone who was once bitten by a dog may panic when confronted by a harmless puppy. To him, that puppy represents danger.

It is only natural for parents to be controlling. Parents who raised a child from infancy may indeed understand logically that he or she is now a mature adult, but the emotion may persist that this grown up is still a child in need of care and guidance.

Once, while in Canada, my father was visited by an eighty-six-year-old man who hailed from the village that was my father's birthplace. After a bit, the man asked, "Rabbi, would you mind visiting my father?"

My father was surprised that an eighty-six-year-old man had a living father. "He denies his age," the man said. "He says he is one hundred twelve. The truth is, he is one hundred fourteen."

My father seized the opportunity to visit this centenarian, who remembered my father's ancestors of six generations earlier. Even at this advanced age, the man's mind was clear. He asked my father, "Did my boychickl come to see you?" To a father, an eighty-six-year-old man was still a boychickl.

As I pointed out earlier, when emotion conflicts with logic, emotion often wins. Parents may act toward grown up sons or daughters as if they were still children.

When a child marries, the parents gain a son or daughter. By the same token, they also lose a son or daughter. Until now, they were essentially the principal recipient of their child's affection and attention. Now the lion's share of affection and attention is going to go to the spouse, and they will get the crumbs. That's how they feel, and that is a loss. Can we blame them for wanting to hold on?

Although the children do not want to hurt their parents, the fact is that by getting married and diverting their affection and attention from them, they are doing just that, and they may feel guilty, as though they had committed a crime. They may like to spend weekends alone, but feel guilty if they do so. The parents may give them the "good news" that they are going on vacation and are giving them a gift by having bought tickets for them to come along. The young couple does not want to go with them, but refusing will hurt them, and they feel guilty if they do.

When the young couple expresses the idea that they want to have a life of their own, they feel guilty. This is magnified if the parents did not have much in their lives except caring for their children, and they now feel unfulfilled. Should the young couple sacrifice their happiness to avoid hurting their parents and feeling guilty? If so, how much sacrifice is appropriate? Too much sacrifice may generate anger, and the anger may be turned against the spouse.

A simple rule: Sacrifice for parents is appropriate. Sacrificing *the marriage* for parents is not. It takes keen judgment to know the difference.

Parents may meddle because they care. As I mentioned earlier, an unwise statement by a doctor when I was ten caused my father to believe that I had heart disease, and he was very overprotective of me. After I was married and my father found out that I had a fever, he repeatedly checked whether my wife had called the doctor, whether I was taking my medicine regularly, whether the house was warm enough, whether I was drinking adequate hot tea, etc. My wife was a bit offended that he would think of her as being so incompetent, but to my father, his darling child was dangerously ill, and he was worried whether this young woman was capable enough of giving his child the care that he had given him all those years. The reaction could be either a gentle reassurance or a hostile response to being accused of being inept. An understanding of where he was coming from made the difference.

On the first Friday that we were alone, after my wife had prepared for Shabbos a box was delivered containing challah, gefilte fish, chicken soup, roast chicken, kugel and cake. We had a good laugh over it. My wife called my mother to thank her, and we put the food in the freezer. How was my mother to know that this young woman knew anything about cooking? And if she was able to cook, how would she know what foods her little boy likes? Without empathy, this kind gesture could have been interpreted as an insult.

As a young couple, you might wish to spend a quiet Shabbos alone, but your parents insist that you must be with them for Shabbos. Would you rather that they didn't want you? Most parents love to have their children with them for Shabbos. Just wait. When *your* children get married you will feel the same way. A good response is, "We love to be with you for Shabbos, but next Shabbos we'll be at our home. We need some alone time." If it is technically feasible, occasionally (but very occasionally) you might say, "How about your coming to *us* for Shabbos?" That would also give you a chance to prove that you know how to make chicken soup.

You want to buy furniture for your apartment. Mother-in-law comes along to make sure you buy the right furniture. "I have to help the kids choose furniture. They don't know quality or prices." She's probably right. If they are paying for the furniture, they may feel that this gives them the right to choose it. You may be tempted to say, "Look, who's going to be living with this furniture, you or me?" You'd be better off saying, "Mom, I'm so glad you're going to guide me on quality and prices, but our tastes may differ. You might like traditional, but I like more contemporary. But I do want your help on quality and prices." If you reject their help outright and buy what you like, do not be surprised if, disapproving of the drapes you bought, they say, "Look at the *shmattes* (rags) they have hanging on the windows!" Of course, this is petty and it is much preferred that they respect your choice for your own home.

However, even if they respond negatively try to understand where they are coming from.

Then a baby comes along. "Good heavens! What does this nineteen-year-old girl know about taking care of a baby? Why, she's just a baby herself! My precious grandchild! I've raised six children. I have to help her with her first child." Don't take offense. Furthermore, she may have a point. You might say, "Mom, I appreciate all your help, but I have to follow the pediatrician's instructions."

Your mother-in-law might want to show you how to bathe the baby. Let her do it the first time, then say, "Mom, I want you to watch me and see if I'm doing it right."

The arrival of a child can do much for cementing relationships with in-laws. Until now they were only your husband's/wife's parents. In the grandchild, both sets of grandparents participate in the one person. This can be unifying.

If you've married the oldest child in the family, there is yet another consideration. This is the first time they are parents-in-law. They were probably no more prepared to become parents-in-law than you were to become a husband, wife or parent. Give them a break. They've got to learn.

If you've married the youngest child in the family, there may be yet another problem. Your in-laws now have to deal with the "empty nest syndrome." That can be quite traumatic. Parents who have spent most of their adult life caring for their children suddenly find themselves with no one to take care of. If they are not both occupied with work, this may hit hard. They may be unable to let go. Give them this consideration. It will take some time for them to adjust. What you see as meddling is just their way of trying to be useful. It can be very depressing to feel useless. You may have to wean them gradually from their emotional dependence on you.

There may be factors in your in-laws' background that you are unaware of that affects their behavior. If they were Holocaust survivors or children of survivors they may have emotions that you cannot understand. Or, they may have gone through difficult times early in their marriage. It is helpful to say, "Mom and Dad, this is so new to us. Can you tell us something about how things were for you when you were first married?" This may get you brownie points. They may be more than happy to tell you about their ordeals, and it may also help you understand where they're coming from.

Never, but never, bad-mouth your in-laws to your spouse. She may know their shortcomings, but they are her parents, and they should be treated respectfully. However, you do have to work together on this. Don't put your spouse on the defensive. She may not feel that the parents are intrusive. You may say, "Honey, do you feel your parents are not giving us enough space?" If your spouse says, "No, I don't think so," you have planted the idea, and your spouse may come around to realizing it. When an incident occurs which you see as intrusive, point it out gently. A concrete example is more convincing than a generality.

Your parents' and in-laws' behavior may appear unreasonable to you. If you can empathize, it will not be unreasonable. You may not approve of it, but you will handle it differently if you do not accuse them of being unreasonable.

Assuming that there are two sets of parents-in-law, there may be a conflict of loyalties. One set of in-laws may feel that the children are spending an unfair amount of time with the other in-laws. It is not unheard of that they may demand equal time, down to the hour. Sometimes this can be most unreasonable. One woman said, "We lived just a few blocks from my husband's parents, but my parents lived in another city. If we spent a weekend at my parents' home, my in-laws insisted that we must stay at their home for a weekend. We could have easily walked over for the meals, but no, we had to pack up our clothes and the kids' clothes. It was so unnecessary, but that's just the way they are." Another woman said, "My mother-in-law said, 'You spent eight hours at your husband's parents but only five hours with us.'"

If in-laws are unreasonable in this way, it is unlikely that you will satisfy them regardless of what you do, so it may be futile to try.

Plan well in advance for the holidays. Both your parents and in-laws may take for granted that you are going to be with them for the Seder, and it will come as a shock to them that you want to be with your spouse's parents. So about Chanukah time, tell your parents or in-laws, "Mendy and I (or Chaya and I) decided that were going to be at his parents for the Seder and with you the second days." Don't say "O.K.?" You and your spouse *decided*, and you have a right to that decision.

You and your spouse should reach the decision about how much time you are going to spend with either set of in-laws by discussing it between yourselves. You can then decide which of you is going to tell the parents about the decision, *when* you are going to tell them and *how* you will tell them. Plan on how to respond to their reaction. The first time you tell them of your decision, it may hit them like a blockbuster. It is your "Declaration of Independence." They may swallow hard and take it gracefully, or they may say, "Well, if that's the way it's going to be, just forget about us. You don't have to speak to us again." It is conceivable that they may even say, "If you want to be on your own, then do it all the way. Don't expect us to support you." When you make your decision to declare your independence, you should consider all the possible ramifications. Remember the difference we made between "reacting" and "responding." They may *react*, but you should *respond.*

If parents react with, "Then just forget about us," you may say, "We're sorry you're taking it that way. We'll *never* forget about you. We love you and we want to be with you. We welcome your advice, but we must make our own decisions." Don't fret that they will never talk to you again. They don't want to lose their children, and after the initial reaction wears off, they'll come around.

Once you've made the decision, support each other. As kids, we sometimes play one parent against the other. Now it's their turn to do so. Don't let it happen. You should relate to parents and in-laws as "we" rather than "I."

Always be respectful to your parents and in-laws. You may disagree with them, but do so respectfully.

Of course, there may be extremes. Parents and parents-in-law may be smothering, and their intrusiveness may just be intolerable. Even after you empathize, they still seem unreasonable. They may want to control ever facet of your life. If they are intractable, get some counseling from someone *with established competence* in parental and in-law relationships on how to handle this. Not every purveyor of advice, regardless of their degrees, is competent in family matters, so look for someone capable. Do not rely on your own judgment. You may have a knee-jerk reaction and say or do something for which you will never be forgiven. But do not ignore the problem in the hope that it will go away on its own. Your spouse may love you very much, but also has loyalty to his parents, and if the issues are not resolved, it may cause friction between the two of you. This must be avoided. It is not wise to tell your spouse, "You have to tell your parents that they are too intrusive." That puts your spouse in the middle and causes him to be pulled in two directions. Get good counseling, and present a united front.

If your parents happen to be supporting you early in the marriage and assume that because they are paying the bills they have the right to call all the shots, you should reconsider your options. You might tell them that while you truly appreciate their help, their attitude is causing some problems. Suggest that all of you see a counselor together to work out proper boundaries. If they reject this and are frankly dominating because they are supporting you and will not let go, you may have to seriously consider revamping your plans so that you can detach yourself to some degree from their support. This may seem impossible to you, but if the choice is between changing your plans or having your marriage wrecked, you may have to make the impossible more possible.

Children have an obligation to honor their parents. It is one of the Ten Commandments. However, the same Torah that commands this said right at the beginning, "Therefore shall a man leave his father and mother and cleave to his wife" (*Genesis* 2:24). If push comes to shove, the obligation to one's spouse and children takes priority.

Esther consulted me because as much as she loved her husband, the marriage was in jeopardy. Nathan's mother was a widow and made many demands on him. Nathan was busy at the office all week. He invited his mother for Shabbos, but she said that she prefers to remain home. On Sunday morning she would call that she needs the lawn mowed or some other chore done. Although Sunday was the only day that they could have some family activities, Nathan would leave his wife and children and go to his mother.

When Nathan and Esther would go out for dinner, Nathan would invite his mother, although Esther wanted some "alone" time. Nathan's mother generally refused, saying, "No, you and Esther go and have a good time. I can stay home." Nathan did *not* have a good time at all. Throughout dinner, he was consumed with guilt that his mother was home alone.

I suggested to Nathan to consult a *halachic* authority to find out what his Torah obligations were. The rabbi told him that while he must be respectful of his mother, his prime obligation was to his wife. He might offer to pay someone to cut the grass or do other things that his mother wanted, but he must devote himself primarily to his wife and children.

Following the rabbi's instructions not only saved the marriage, but also had a salutary effect on Nathan's mother. She became involved in a nearby senior citizen's center and developed new relationships, which she would not have done had Nathan continued to respond to her every call.

Proper counseling, as in this case, can preserve a marriage and make it a much happier one.

Just a few words to parents-in-law: Respect that your children have now become a family of their own. Do not conclude that they favor the other in-laws over you. They may have valid reasons why they are allotting their time the way they do, and their division of time should not be seen as an indicator of how much they love you. Respect their decisions. Do not set the couple against each other by playing on their loyalties.

Whatever it is that you are giving your children, give it whole-heartedly with no strings attached. If you want your children to have something, give it lovingly. Do not expect to be paid back for what you have given. Your children should be grateful for what you give them, but do not use gifts as an instrument of control.

The Controlling Parent

As noted, it is not easy for parents who were under the impression that they had control of their child, to adjust to the reality that this is not true. They may wish to exert the control at twenty that they felt they had in infancy.

I have often quipped that if I were to see any of my children going to a support group for "Children of Dysfunctional Parents," my reaction would be, "Thank G-d! They've found a place to get help."

Was I a dysfunctional parent? Look at it this way. At the age of seventy-plus, having learned much from life's experiences and educational sources, my wisdom is at its highest point. But I did not have my children when I had the wisdom of a septuagenarian.

Rather, I had them when I was in my twenties, when I did not have this mature wisdom. Of course I must have been dysfunctional. Given the relative paucity of wisdom we have when we raise our children, we are *all*, to some degree, dysfunctional.

Our children begin life totally helpless. They could not survive without our care. The realization that they are growing and maturing has to make inroads on our perception of their helplessness and dependence on us.

Consciously, we wish our children to become independent. We educate them and train them with the goal that they should become self-sufficient and not be forever dependent on us. We may even resent prolonged dependence. We hope and pray that our children will survive us, and failure to achieve independence from us would leave them helplessly stranded.

That is logic. Logic operates in the conscious mind. The subconscious does not operate on logical principles, and the feelings that reside in the subconscious can be totally illogical. Yet, they are very real and may exert a powerful influence on our thoughts and behavior.

When our children are young and are dependent on us, we feel useful. When they eventually achieve total self-sufficiency and can detach from us, we may be happy for them and proud that we have accomplished our task as parents. Yes, we may be happy *consciously*, but the subconscious that equated their dependence on us with a feeling of usefulness may not share in that happiness.

Bernice was a widow whose divorced daughter, Sandra, and her eight-year-old son lived with her. She prepared meals for them, did their laundry and made her grandson's lunch every school day.

One day Sandra returned home with good news. Her fiancé had been given a significant promotion at work with an increase in salary that would enable them to get married. He had been appointed division head of the company's branch in another city.

Bernice congratulated her daughter and was happy for her, but she felt a pang of sadness. If Sandra and her son moved away, what function would she have? What would there be to look forward to upon awakening in the morning? But how dare she feel sad? This was a wonderful opportunity for her daughter, and Harold was indeed a wonderful man. Bernice struggled to free herself of the feeling of sadness. She felt guilty being sad when she should be happy for Sandra. She felt terrible that her selfish feelings and her possessiveness of Sandra and her grandson stood in the way of sharing her daughter's joy.

Bernice had difficulty falling asleep that night. She awoke at 3 a.m. with shortness of breath and chest pain. She woke Sandra, who immediately called 911. Bernice was hospitalized in the intensive care unit. For the next two days she was hooked up to a monitor and underwent a battery of blood tests. On the third day, while Sandra was visiting, the doctor said to Bernice, "I have good news for you. Your heart is healthy and all your blood tests are normal. There is nothing wrong with you, and you may go home."

Bernice began crying. Sandra said, "Why are you crying, Mom? Everything is O.K. The doctor said that there is nothing wrong with you."

All that the doctor could know was that Bernice's tests were normal. What he did not know was that there was something very much wrong with her. She had lost her reason for living.

Parents need to be needed. They may not be able to feel that they are needed when their children detach from them.

Many years after I was independent of my parents, I needed them very much. I needed their "mazal tov" when a child was born. I needed someone to call and to be happy for me when the baby had his first tooth and took his first steps. I needed them to tell me how beautiful the pictures of the children were. I needed them at the Bar Mitzvzahs. I missed my father at my children's weddings. I was fortunate that my mother could share in my *simchas* (happy occasions), and it was a very sad day when I could no longer call her with some good tidings about the grandchildren. Parents never outgrow their usefulness, but many do not know that.

Someone defined *love* as "the ability to understand someone even if you disagree with him." Remember the importance of empathy, of being able to see things from another person's perspective. Your parents do not have control over their subconscious, and they may not be aware that feelings in their subconscious are influencing the way they think and act.

In your parents' subconscious there are still vivid images of when you ran into the street to retrieve your rubber ball, and when you cried bitterly because you were not allowed to buy an ice cream a half hour before supper. Consciously, they know that you are mature and responsible, but these lingering impressions may raise some doubts as to the soundness of your decisions. It may take some time until the effects of these subconscious feelings may be overcome.

Incidentally, you, too, have a subconscious which is refractory to logic, and it, too, may retain ancient memories. You may have resented parental control at age five. Twenty-five years later, your parent makes a rather innocent comment which is not controlling, but your subconscious feelings are triggered by this comment and you may react to it as if it was an attempt to control you.

Just because you resent parental control does not mean that, in some way, you may not still long for it. When my father was weakened by cancer and had to physically lean on me to go to the doctor's office, I felt that the world had turned upside-down. For me to lean on my father would have been more natural. For him to lean on me was very painful to me. At that point I would have been glad if he had been well enough to control me.

In the 1960's, there was a cultural revolution, with the emergence of the conviction that anyone over thirty is obsolete, and wisdom resides in youth. We have not recovered from that disastrous era. Psychiatrists specializing in treatment of adolescents report that the most frequent diagnosis they make is "Oppositional Defiant Disorder," which essentially means disagreeing with parents simply because they are parents. Unfortunately, this has often resulted in tragic consequences.

At age twenty-two, I received *semichah* (ordination) and became assistant to my father in his shul. The first time I had to officiate at a funeral and deliver a eulogy, my father asked me,

"What are you going to say?" I felt the blood rushing to my head. If my judgement is not good enough, I should not have been given the position. If you took me in this position, you should trust my judgement. I felt infuriated.

I told my father what I had prepared for the eulogy, and he made some corrections. How foolish it was of me to have resented his sage advice! I had an excellent opportunity to learn from him, but with the omniscience of a young adult, I did not realize how valuable this opportunity was.

Was my father being controlling? Perhaps, but it was constructive control. Much of what children may see as control by a parent may actually be guidance which should not be dismissed.

Eventually, my father stopped asking me what I had prepared to say in a sermon. Rather, he was excited with anticipation that my sermon would be good.

The overwhelming majority of parents want to be good parents. Most probably, they raise their children the way they were raised. That is really the only training they had. If they had a controlling parent, they are likely to repeat that pattern.

It is a good idea to ask your parents, "What was it like when you were a child or adolescent?" Not only will you get insights into their behavior, but in relating this, they may see that they are repeating things that they resented.

Young children may react to parental control in a variety of ways. They may be "passive-aggressive," not openly defying their parents but finding ways to avoid complying with their wishes. Or, they may be "super-good," to earn their parents' love, and perhaps to show how much better they are than a sibling. Once traits like these begin in childhood, they may persist into adolescence and adulthood. It may be very helpful to do some self-examination and see how you reacted to parental control earlier in life. If you can identify this, you may be able to modify your attitude and behavior.

You might ask your parents whether they ever disagreed with *their* parents, and how things turned out. At some point, you may wish to say, "Dad or Mom, I know you have my best interest at heart. I really want your input, because I know that you have wisdom that I don't have. But after I have your input, I'm going to have to make my own decisions. I may make mistakes, but that's the only way I'll learn. I do want you to know that I value your suggestions, even when I don't follow them."

There may be cases of parental control that are excessive and intolerable. Surrendering to control is a mistake, but acting in defiance may not be better. Consult someone with expertise in parent/child relationships on how to handle your particular situation.

The Controlling Child

Small children feel themselves under parental control, and they do not like it. Remember Antonine's observation? The *yetzer hara* does not wish to be restrained, and if it inhabited a fetus, it would kick its way out of the mother's womb, preferring death to being restrained. The *yetzer hara* does enter a person at birth, and from there on, for the rest of the person's life, it battles against restraint. The *yetzer tov* (good inclination) does not come about until Bar or Bas Mitzvah. By then the *yetzer hara* has ruled for thirteen or twelve years without opposition.

The *yetzer tov* has an uphill battle. Many children enter the adolescent phase *even before* the *yetzer tov* appears on the scene, and they act out their resistance to being controlled. Inasmuch as offense is the best defense, some adolescents try to throw off parental control by *wielding control over their parents.*

Make no mistake about it. Adolescents know how to push their parents' buttons. They know exactly where their parents are most vulnerable. If they are put in a position where they feel they want to control their parents, they know what they must do. The only real way to avoid this is to *raise your children in a way that will minimize their being in such a position.*

The suggestions made in the chapters on parental control may be helpful. But having stressed the importance of empathy, I wish to comment about empathizing with teenagers.

First of all, the institution of "adolescence" is the craziest idea that civilization has come up with. It is totally unnatural.

I was once called to the hospital emergency room to care for an adolescent who had come for help. When I asked the young man what his problem was, he remained silent. After a prolonged period of silence, he said, "I am a nothing."

"Why do you think you're a nothing?" I asked.

"Well, what am I?" he said. "I'm not a child and I'm not an adult. I'm a nothing."

It had not occurred to me previously that adolescence is an unnatural construct. Primitive tribes do not have adolescence. There are puberty rites, at which time a child becomes an adult. Of course, this is so in *halachah.* A young girl of eleven years, 353 days (the Jewish year) is a *ketana* (minor). A young boy of twelve years 353 days is a *katan* (minor). At the moment of sunset on the 354th day, a magic transition occurs. These children become adults. They are competent to make legal contracts. If they commit a crime, they are judged as any adult of forty. There is no "juvenile justice system."

Until the moment of transition, the parents are responsible for a child's behavior. One second after the magic moment, the youngster is fully responsible for his/her behavior.

Along comes civilization's misguided adolescent phase, and we have a period of non-responsibility. You cannot hold the parents responsible for a sixteen-year-old's behavior. He is too big for them to control. You can not hold him responsible, because he is not yet sufficiently mature. Who is responsible for an adolescent's actions? No one! Little wonder that the young man in the emergency considered himself a nothing.

If this no-man's land were not bewildering enough, the young person is further confused about just when he does become an adult. At sixteen to drive a car, but not to buy cigarettes, at eighteen he may buy cigarettes but not liquor, he can be drafted at eighteen but until recently could not vote. At fourteen he may give consent for his own treatment. And just a few miles away, across the state line, there is a different schedule. He may be an adolescent in his home, but twenty-five miles away he is an adult. Is it any wonder that adolescents are thoroughly confused, groping desperately for an identity?

In an effort to become an adult instead of a "nothing," the logic of a sixteen-year-old may be, "Adults may drink alcohol. Hence, by drinking alcohol, I become an adult."

All this time, the adolescent is undergoing a radical physical transformation. Many adolescents feel totally out of place, being either too short or too tall, too developed or underdeveloped. Their hormones are raging. The adult world preaches morality to them and then provokes them with stimuli that drive them nuts.

I am not excusing adolescent misbehavior, but I believe that they do deserve our empathy. As I pointed out earlier, our adolescent children are confronted with unprecedented challenges. We should appreciate this and get the best education available on proper parenting.

Your adolescent child knows how to blackmail you. If she so decides, she can do something which will hurt and embarrass you. In all likelihood, you rather than the youngster may suffer the worst consequences of such acting-out behavior.

Children learn well. *If you tried to control them by intimidation, they may now try to control you by intimidation.*

Children did not always have the degree of control they do today. When I was in grade school, the worst possible thing that could happen was being sent to the principal's office. The walk to the office was replete with anxiety and trepidation. Waiting outside the principal's office was akin to being in death row in prison. There was respect for authority: parents, teachers, police, courts, clergy. Children did not have the faintest notion of controlling their parents.

Today, teachers and principals may fear the students much more than the students fear them. Court orders are regularly defied. Respect for police has dwindled. Parental authority has suffered along with the rest. With the lapse of parental authority, children have seized the initiative.

Those who advocate an authoritative approach to discipline say that rules must be enforced. It is not clear, however, how this can be done. When parents had authority, they could ground a youngster or deny him privileges. Today, a youngster can bolt out of the house. Calling the police rarely accomplishes anything, and you cannot legally evict a twelve-year-old from the house.

Can being controlled by children be prevented? If children are raised with love and understanding, if the atmosphere in the house is one where they learn to respect their parents (primarily because the parents respect each other) and if parents model deference to authority, it is less likely that children will try to control.

Proper parenting techniques may minimize the adolescent's need or desire to control. Some helpful readings are *Discipline That Works* by Dr. Thomas Gordon, *How to Talk So That Kids Will Listen and How to Listen So That Kids Will Talk* by Faber and Mazlish, and *Between Parent and Teenager* by Dr. Hiam Ginott.

If you find yourself being controlled by an adolescent, do not rely on your own wisdom how to manage him/her. Consult someone with expertise on adolescent behavior.

The Difficult Child

Although the discussion about control must address the task of parenting, I make no claim at being an authority on parenting. The book, *Positive Parenting*, was written in collaboration with a very competent child psychologist. However, I must make a few remarks about a special problem that presents a challenge to parents, where a "do-it-yourself" approach of control can be most unfortunate.

There are children who seem to have severe behavior problems from their earliest age. There is reason to believe that these children have been born with difficult temperaments. Even if this is so, it does not mean that they are not manageable. However, raising these children requires expert guidance. Handling these children by the way a parent thinks is best may be a serious mistake.

These children may be very aggressive. They seem to be insensitive to other people's feelings and are totally self-centered. They have no control over their anger and can be violent toward their parents and siblings. They act on impulse, doing whatever they feel like doing, without any logic or reason. It is not that they are not logical, but rather that they use their logic to get what they want or to figure out how to escape punishment if they are caught. To them, what they feel like doing *at the moment* is the most important thing in their lives.

Being insensitive to others' feelings, these children cannot understand why their parents get so upset over what they have done. If they are punished for doing wrong, they do not regret what they have done, and they become frustrated and angry. They see punishment as an unprovoked attack against them. If they are told to do homework or clean up their room they will put it off as long as possible, and if confronted, they may manipulate, lie or throw temper tantrums. They know how to push their parents' buttons and provoke them. They know how to set one parent against the other. If the parents have separated, they know how to put the separation to their own advantage. *They know how to control their parents.* Even the most loving parents may lose their cool with these children.

Parents may try to manage these children by punishment and deprivations. They may try to bribe them to be good. Finding that their methods are ineffective, they may try one thing after another, which results in an inconsistency which can only make matters worse.

An unmanageable child not only causes great anguish to his parents, but his behavior also affects his siblings. He is the focal point of so much of the parents' time that the other children are deprived of the attention they deserve. Perhaps worst of all, the child may grow up with antisocial behavior, resulting in self-destruction as well as harm to others.

There is only one point I wish to make here. If you have a child that fits the above description, *don't try to manage him using your own resources.* Even reading books on parenting may not be enough. At the first sign that the child is impulsive, self-centered and refractory to discipline at an age when he should be responding to discipline, *get help!* Find a competent child therapist and follow instructions! Don't blame the child's behavior on the other parent. In a two-parent home, *both* parents should go for guidance and present a united front.

With proper guidance from a competent child therapist, these children can be brought around to normal behavior.

What About the Boss?

I n many relationships, but particularly in the workplace, the feelings we have toward other people may be the result of earlier experiences.

We relate to reality according to our perceptions of reality, and these may not be the same for everyone. Sure, two people who look at a tree are likely to have the same perception of the tree. But two people who work for the same employer may have widely divergent perceptions of him.

One person had a father who was gentle and considerate of his feelings. When his father wanted him to do something, he spoke softly and gave clear instructions of what he wanted. If he did things right, his father acknowledged it. If he made a mistake, the father corrected him, pointing out what was wrong and why. He loved and respected his father.

The other person's father was cold and aloof. He gave the children orders like a general, sometimes barking at them. When children obeyed his orders, he never commended them for it. If they made a mistake, he could fly into a rage, insulting them and disparaging them. He may have hit them if he thought them to be disobedient. The children feared the father more than they loved him.

To these people, an authority figure, a superior or an employer is in the position of a father. They may not see this person for what he is. Their perception has been tainted by their early life experiences with an authority figure. One may see the boss or manager as a considerate leader or adviser, and the other may see him as an ogre.

The workplace is also a site where one may transfer feelings that one had toward siblings to coworkers. One may see them as helpful and friendly, or one may see them as fierce competitors.

In all relationships, but particularly in the workplace, it is wise to remember that we may be relating to people with preconceived notions about them.

O.K. You're working for a company. You may be answerable to the CEO or to a division head. How did these people get to these positions? Unless they were the heirs of the founder, they got there by striving for success at all costs, driving others to outdo the competition, trying to be perfect, trying to look good and accepting responsibilities. The very traits that catapulted them into being the boss are those that make a person a controller.

O.K., you may understand that. But your boss is driving you nuts by constantly badgering you, constantly checking up on you, repeatedly instructing you to do things his way and refusing to listen to your suggestions. Sometimes this becomes so unbearable that you want to tell him off and quit, but you can't do that because you do not have any other job prospect readily available. So instead you come home grumpy and take it out on the wife and the kids.

Here is a piece of information that may help you better understand the boss and it may also help you discover something about yourself.

As was noted, successful executives may get to their positions by assertiveness and aggressiveness. Think of it this way. You are driving along level land and come to a very steep hill. In order to get up the hill, you must shift into a more powerful gear. After you get to the top of the hill, you are again on level terrain. You wish to switch back to a cruising gear, but the shift is stuck. You have no choice but to travel in the more powerful gear.

The problem is that the more powerful gear cannot reach cruising speeds. It is suitable for a steep climb, but it cannot exceed thirty miles/hour. You cannot travel fast and furthermore, you may wear out the gear by driving long distances.

Similarly, it may require competitiveness and aggressiveness to build up a business. Once this has been achieved, one should be able to switch into "cruising speed." But work habits are hard to break. Although the degree of aggressiveness necessary to get to the top is no longer appropriate, one may not be able to "switch gears." Using the same techniques one had used in climbing may actually be counterproductive, but it is difficult to change one's habits.

If bosses realized that their control can be counterproductive, perhaps they might relinquish some control. Employees who have some leeway and flexibility are generally happier at work, and their attitude can increase productivity. Studies have demonstrated that employees who are not dominated by a controlling superior have a lesser incidence of coronary heart disease. This alone can make them more valuable over the long run.

However, do not bank on the boss realizing this.

What can you do to keep both your job and your sanity? Let's begin with empathy. Suppose you were the boss, how different would you be? Don't forget, the buck stops at his desk. He is ultimately responsible for everything that his subordinates do. That generates enough anxiety to want to be in control of everything. His attitude may be, "I have to stay on top of things. One slip-up and my goose is cooked."

When I became director of the Department of Psychiatry of St. Francis Hospital, I was under a great deal of stress. The demands for service were incessant, and I had to carry the load. On a good night, I was awoken only seven times by nurses or by the emergency room staff. On a bad night, I was awoken fifteen times.

Then Congress passed the Mental Health Act and funded Community Mental Health Centers. Having received a sizable sum of money, I hired several psychiatrists, psychologists and social workers. Alas, the stress increased rather than decreased. Previously, I had been responsible for only my own actions. Now I was also responsible for those of a large staff.

One day, the administrator met me leaving the hospital. "You look very tired, Dr. Twerski. Perhaps we can get you an assistant." I said, "Sister, one more assistant and I quit!"

Although the staff was competent, it was my neck that was on the block. A wrong medication or the mismanagement of a suicidal threat could result in a serious malpractice suit, in which I, as clinical director, could be held liable. I had to check the medications and disposition of many cases. If the staff felt that I was too controlling, well, that was just too bad.

If your boss is too controlling, think of his position and picture yourself in his place.

After a while, I could see which of the staff was totally reliable, and I did very little checking on them. Look for ways in which the boss will be able to see that you are competent and do not need monitoring. Try to anticipate his monitoring. If you know he is likely to check up on an assignment, try to complete it ahead of schedule and bring it to him. "Here's the report on the Johnston case, Mr. Evans. I think everything is in order, but would you mind looking it over?"

When I served my internship in medicine, I found out who the chief of medicine was on the first day. He was a perfectionist, if not obsessive-compulsive. He was to be my boss for a whole year. Could I put up with it?

I spent an extra hour every day in the medical library, looking up articles in the medical literature about some of the more difficult cases. I photocopied them and gave them to the chief. When I had to report to him on a case, you had better believe I knew everything there was to know about the patient's medical and family history. It took two months for him to build up trust in me, but the rest of the year was a breeze. It was very gratifying when one day he asked me to gather all the information I could about a case that he was to present at a medical conference. I must admit that as difficult as it was to have a compulsive, controlling superior, I probably learned more about medicine than if the chief had been more easy going.

When I had my surgery rotation, there was one surgeon who was a controller, but rather than being afraid of being humiliated or sued for a mistake, I could see that he was genuinely interested in his patients and wanted to make sure that they got the best care. Once I realized his motivation, it was much easier to accept his control.

Back in medical school days, there was an instructor who insisted that our patient work-ups be done in a certain format, which I thought was extra work for no good reason. I gently said, "Dr. Murphy, wouldn't it be better if we did it this way?" His answer was curt and firm. "Twerski, when you run a department, you can do it your way. Here, you do it my way."

I must share something with you. In Torah observance, we do not understand everything we are required to do. There are *chukim*, laws for which there may be no logical reason. When I buy a wool garment, I have it tested for possible admixture of linen, and if it is found, it must be removed. Why? Because that is what the Torah says. Why does the Torah say that? I do not know, but I must accept Torah authority. This was good training for me to accept authority even if I did not understand the reason for the orders.

After all is said and done, some bosses are really impossible. Consider your options. Can you walk away from the job? If not, look for ways to unwind (without alcohol) so that you do not pour your wrath out at home. Let your wife know the stress you are under. There are some books on relaxation exercises in the self-help section of the bookstore. Relaxation techniques do work.

If you do quit, do so courteously. Do not seize the opportunity to ventilate all your pent up anger at the boss. Remember, a subsequent employer is going to call him for references on you. Do not shoot yourself in the foot.

One accountant simply could not put up with his boss's constant checking every minute detail. He sought another job, and when he was assured of having it, he met with the boss.

"I am here to tell you that I have an offer with another firm. I've been here eight years, and I know the company thoroughly. It'll take you a while to break in a new person.

"The reason that I'm leaving is because your constant standing over me and checking up on me has become intolerable. By now you should have been assured that I am reliable. If in spite of that assurance you still have to check up on me, I think that means that you have a problem delegating responsibilities and you are uneasy unless you are personally on top of everything. I imagine that must be pretty hard on you, but you can't help yourself.

"Maybe it's not my business to tell you about your personality. It is no longer a problem for me, because I have another job waiting for me. I'm sure some other employees feel the way I do. If you can do something to get over the need of being personally on top of everything, you'll have much happier employees."

The boss sat in silence for a few minutes, then said, "I think you're right, Sam, and I appreciate your telling me. I know I am a perfectionist and have trouble delegating. I'm bothered by the uncertainty that things are done right. I didn't realize how much it is affecting others.

"I may not be able to change overnight, but I'm going to try. I'd really like you to stay with us, and if you can manage to put up with me while I try to change, I'd be very grateful."

This particular episode had a happy ending for everyone.

The student/teacher relationship is another one that invites control. The student is really at the mercy of the teacher. If he gives you a bad grade, there is usually no appeal.

In my pre-medicine courses, I was running an "A" in biochemistry all semester. Somehow, I did not do too well on the final exam, and it brought my final grade down to 91.4, which is a "B." In those days, the admission committee judged applicants for medical school solely by their grades. The more "A's" one had, the better was the chance of getting accepted.

I asked the instructor if she could raise the grade to "A." After all, I was above 93 all semester. She said that if the final grade had been 92.4, she would have done it, but 91.4 remains a "B." I told her that this 1.6 difference may determine whether or not I get accepted to medical school, and that my whole life career rests on that tiny numerical difference. She shrugged and said that she was sorry, but that the numbers speak for themselves. I said, "I understand." I did not argue with her and I did not go to the department head.

That night I got a call from her at home. "I changed it to an 'A,' Twerski. Good luck in medical school."

Try to stay on the good side of the teacher. This is much easier to do, because in contrast to an employer, this teacher will probably not be your boss the next semester. A few months is tolerable.

In any relationship, boss, teacher or peer, it may ease things if you can find out what the controlling person's interests are. If he is a golfer, ask him about golf. If he is a stamp collector, ask him about stamps. One of my professors was keen on the history of medicine, something which is generally not covered in the average medical school. I took out a book on the history of medicine, which was, incidentally, quite interesting. I then asked him a few questions, which gave him the opportunity to show me how much he knew about the subject. It's surprising how controlling people may relinquish some control when you make them an authority.

What? Friends, Too?

Yes. Friends and peers may be "control freaks." I had a colleague who frequently said, "Abe, can you help me out and take call for me?" He then came up with a pathetic reason why he could not take call that night. I would feel like a heel if I refused.

Sometimes peers take advantage. In the army, two officers shared an office. One took things easy, resting his feet on the desk and reading a magazine, while the other always had a tall stack in the "IN" box.

One day the busy one asked the other officer, "What's your secret? I can barely finish my work by the end of the day, and you're always at leisure."

The other officer said, "It's simple. When something comes across my desk, I write on it 'Bring to the attention of Major Smith.' In a base as large as this, there's got to be a Major Smith."

"How dare you!" the busy officer exclaimed. "I'm Major Smith."

Sometimes a person may be so totally controlled at home by a bossy and even abusive spouse that he looks for ways to assert some authority. In psychology this is referred to as "identification with the aggressor." If it does not inconvenience you too much, you may humor him. If he really imposes on you, tell him in a gentle way why you can not comply with his request. Do not be afraid of losing a friend. This person is likely to act similarly with all his friends, and many of them will just avoid him. He cannot afford to lose you.

I suggest that you do not tell other friends, "Jim is really making a pest of himself." They may be your friends, but some people cannot resist telling Jim, "You know what Bill said about you?" even though this involves a grievous sin of *rechilus* (carrying tales).

Friends who are controlling may not pose too much of a problem socially. You do not have to meet them more often than you wish. It's another thing when your coworker is a control freak. That can be a daily day occurrence and can be very annoying. You may keep your annoyance under control until it exceeds the boiling point, at which time you may have a volcanic eruption. That doesn't do anyone any good.

There are some people who are "know-it-alls," and feel that this qualifies them to instruct people. One young man conveyed that between him and his father, they knew everything that was to be known. This was tolerable because we had infrequent social contact. My wife and I would joke about it. We would intentionally introduce far-out subjects to elicit a comment about how much he or his father knew about it. "You know, there is reason to believe that the clouds on Venus may conceal an advanced civilization." Then we would sit back and hear him pontificate on a subject about which neither he nor his father knew anything. It was sort of fun. But if he were a coworker, it would have been intolerable rather than humorous.

Even here empathy has a place. People who are "know-it-alls" and who make sure that you are aware of it are invariably people with low self-esteem. They are desperately trying to escape their feelings of inadequacy by showing how great they really are. I feel sorry for them, and I may not be quite as irritated by someone whom I pity.

Sometimes you can head off their demonstration of omniscience by saying something that will boost their ego. See if you can find something positive about them. "Wow! You finished that work assignment in record time," or even, "That tie is really handsome." At coffee break, ask their opinion about something, whether it be sports or politics or anything that indicates that you respect their knowledge. This does not always work, but sometimes the results are amazing. When they feel they are appreciated, they may not have to resort to control to feel good about themselves.

If your coworker is in the habit of telling you how to do things, you might try asking his advice about a new process. This, too, is an ego boost.

If nothing works and the annoyance is more than you can bear, you may just have to make your friend aware of it. A doctor on my staff who was also a personal friend took the liberty of walking into my office at any time without knocking on the door. I finally had to say, "Alvin, I love you dearly. Sometimes you walk in when I'm on the phone discussing a very private matter, and I don't like to tell you to leave. Please knock before you come in. If I'm not doing something which can't be interrupted, I'm happy to see you."

If you tell your coworker exactly what he is doing that bugs you, he may react defensively, but will eventually come around.

Dr. Parrott makes an important point. He says that the attempt to control may be the way a person tries to ward off anxiety. Being in control of something, almost anything, may ameliorate anxiety.

The Midrash states that after King Solomon was cast from his throne by Ashmedai, he wandered around the country exclaiming, "I am Solomon," but, of course, no one believed him. The Talmud states that whereas Solomon had previously been the ruler of an empire, he was now ruler only over his walking cane (*Sanhedrin* 20b). R' Chaim Shmuelevitz says that Solomon survived this crushing period because he never lost the feeling that he was king. Even if he was only king over his walking cane, he was nevertheless in control of something. Being in control may give a person a feeling of security.

Dr. Parrott states that because today's workplace is so uncertain, with downsizing and layoffs occurring frequently, it is, therefore, an anxious place. Coworkers may try to reduce their anxiety by trying to control.

As noted, some people may try to boost their lagging self-esteem by controlling others. As the workplace becomes more complex and sophisticated, some workers may feel increasingly incompetent. They may feel threatened that they may be replaced by a younger person who is more adept at operating the advanced computers upon which almost everything today depends. Their controlling behavior is reassuring to them. "I must be competent, otherwise I would not be in control."

If you have to correct a coworker, be careful that you do not do so in a way that may aggravate his feelings of incompetence. You might start by asking him to show you how something is done, and then say, "Oh! I thought that this way might be better. What do you think?"

Criticizing a control freak is apt to intensify his controlling behavior. Use tact and diplomacy. My father used to tell me about a woman whose use of tact was absolutely brilliant.

This woman was married to a rabbi who was a fine person and an accomplished scholar, but who was very unfamiliar with worldly matters. His position required him to settle disputes among litigants, and he was very inept in this. Recognizing this shortcoming in her husband, she said to him, "Whenever you mediate or judge in a dispute, always give yourself a chance to think it through. Tell the litigants that you want to sleep on it and that you'll give them your decision the next day."

Whenever there was a dispute in the rabbi's study, the wife eavesdropped and overheard all the details of the argument. The rabbi told the litigants to return the next day for his ruling.

At dinner that night, the wife would say to the rabbi, "I heard some commotion in your study today. What was that all about?"

The rabbi would say, "Oh, there was some bickering between these two people about dissolving their partnership."

The wife, who already knew both sides of the argument, would say, "I'm curious about these things. Do you mind telling me what they were arguing about?"

The rabbi would tell her the essence of the case. "This man took the other man into his business as a partner several years ago, and he now wants to dissolve the partnership. He is asking for a payout of fifty percent. The original proprietor says that he built up the business and doesn't want to give him more than thirty percent. The other man says that in these few years he contributed heavily to the growth of the business."

After a few moments, the wife would say, "I know what you're thinking. You want him to payout thirty-five percent immediately, and then they should analyze the growth of the business during the years of the partnership. After they bring these figures to you, you will determine how much over the thirty-five percent he has coming. Hm! I think you've got a good idea there."

The rabbi never caught on that she had planted the idea in his mind, and indeed assumed it was his own. He eventually developed a reputation as a most sagacious mediator and magistrate! Now, that's tact!

Incidentally, my father told me that this couple had a good marriage. Although she had to guide him in certain areas, she respected him for his character and scholarship.

Tact is indispensable whether you are relating to a control freak or whether you are instructing someone, so that you do not come across as a control freak. If you do not use tact, and you tell a control freak, "Stop telling me what to do! I know what I'm doing," you will undermine whatever relationship you have with him, and this "put down" will only increase his attempts to control.

A Very Tragic Control

As was noted, with the exception of the good kind of control, which is self-control, and the prudent, judicious use of proper discipline or instruction, wielding control is virtually always destructive. Control may be especially destructive and tragic when it occurs in the dissolution of a marriage.

If, after thorough evaluation and consultation, it is determined that a couple should divorce, then it is to everyone's advantage that the divorce proceed as amicably as possible. Unfortunately, one or both partners may have hostile feelings, and the divorce process becomes a battleground. In such cases, the negative traits which a person may have may come to the fore, and various aspects of the divorce proceedings become subject to control issues. The partners may be so affected by their feelings that they are unable to see the damage that they are doing to themselves and, worst of all, to their children.

Children do not come into the world of their own accord. Parents bring children into the world and they, therefore, have the responsibility to give their children the best opportunity to achieve happiness. Nothing in the world can absolve parents from this responsibility. Regardless of how deeply hurt or harmed a spouse may have been, this does not allow one to act it a way that is detrimental to the children's welfare. How the two partners wish to deal with each other in matters that do not affect the children is for them to choose. However, insofar as the children's welfare is concerned, all other considerations must be set aside.

It is deplorable that the parties in a divorce may not only be neglectful of the children's welfare, but may also use the children as a weapon in their battle with each other. *This is an unforgivable sin.*

The parties in a divorce may use control tactics in regard to various issues in a settlement. The ethics and morality of this is a matter of conscience, and if a person wishes to compromise on ethics, that is between him/her and G-d. But they have no right to use children as control. There is nothing as heartbreaking as witnessing the winner of a legal battle gain custody, only to have the children run over and embrace the other spouse, crying, "Don't let them take me away from you." The children's best interest must come first.

The ultimate in nefarious control is when the marriage has ended and the husband refuses to follow the rabbinical instruction to give a *get*. This person is not a "control freak" but rather a "control monster." *Halachah* does require the husband to give the *get*, and to abuse this *halachah* as a weapon for control is a grave violation of the Torah.

We may hear on the news that a person has taken hostages and threatens to kill them if his requests are not met. Holding a wife or children hostage is not any less of an abomination.

It is difficult to conceptualize the dissolution of a marriage as ever being a "win-win" situation. However, if the couple's happiness will indeed be served by their going separate ways, it is conceivable that they may both benefit. However, if the children are negatively affected because of a control battle, then everyone loses, the parents as well as the children.

If there is ever a time when it is mandatory that one totally dismiss control, it is when a marriage ends. Relinquishing the attempt to control at this time is a sign of maturity and "menschlichkeit."

Am I a Control Freak?

This is a question you must ask yourself, but inasmuch as control freaks do not recognize themselves as such, your self-analysis is unreliable. If you have a trusted friend whom you can ask to tell you whether he sees you as controlling, it is a good idea to ask him. You must reassure him that you will be most grateful for an honest assessment, and you must be sincere about this. If you think you will be offended by the truth, don't ask him.

Dr. Parrott has devised a self-test to help you decide if you are a control freak, and if so, of what intensity.

(Reprinted from *The Control Freak* by permission of author, Dr. Les Parrott.)

By answering the following multiple choice questions, you can diagnose your own controlling symptoms. Circle the letter of the response that best represents your reaction. Take as much time as you like, and answer each question honestly.

1. **Some of the items on my lengthy to-do list could be delegated to a family member or a coworker, but**

    A. I don't ask anyone because I don't want to impose.
    B. I feel kind of awkward about it, but I eventually let people know I need help.
    C. I don't hesitate to ask people for help.
    D. I don't see the point of asking, because hardly anyone can do the job as well as I can do it myself.

2. **My family members, friends and coworkers tell me I am sometimes critical and hard to please:**

    A. Never
    B. Sometimes
    C. Frequently
    D. All the time.

3. **When I've taken the time to make plans for an evening with friends and then they want to change what I have arranged,**

    A. I don't say word about it and am happy to go along without making a fuss.
    B. I let them know my feelings, but I eventually change my attitude and go along with it.
    C. I make it clear how hard I worked to pull everything together and try to convince them to see why my way is better.
    D. I make my stance known and don't budge.

4. When I'm having a disagreement with a sales clerk,

A. I swallow my words and give in just to avoid the conflict

B. I work to resolve it as quickly as I can

C. I fight for my point even if it takes some time

D. I often go to the mat to win and show why I'm right.

5. When I'm in a hurry and the driver in front of me is driving especially slowly, causing me to miss green lights,

A. I take that time to slow down and enjoy the ride.

B. I hope he turns off the road so I can get going.

C. I get very frustrated and do whatever I can to pass him.

D. I ride his bumper, flash my lights or honk, and give him a dirty look when I get around him.

6. I'm taking a long overdue vacation with a few friends. When it comes to making travel arrangements and planning our days, my style is to

A. Let my friends do the planning and go with the flow.

B. Offer a couple of suggestions but remain spontaneous.

C. Think through things, like where we will want to eat on that day and plan accordingly.

D. Read up on where we are going, schedule each day ahead of time, and purchase tickets well in advance to avoid potential hassles.

7. In thinking about how people succeed in life,

A. I go with the flow and see what happens.

B. I think it's good to have goals, but everyone has his or her own style.

C. I don't understand people who don't have vision for what they can do.

D. I have little patience for those who simply drift without direction.

8. **I just spent twenty minutes at the office doing absolutely nothing. I feel**

A. Justified. I deserve some slack-off time.
B. Energized. It felt good to veg out.
C. Grumpy. I could have finished a project and not felt so bad.
D. Guilty. I wasted precious time in which I could have gotten more done.

9. **When someone borrows a video from my neatly organized collection and doesn't put the video back in the right order,**

A. It doesn't bother me.
B. I'm just happy the person returned it.
C. I put the video back the way I want it and make a mental note to tell the person where I like it to go.
D. I show the person how to do it right and say that the next time he or she borrows a video, I want it returned to the exact place I have it.

10. **When an important project I've been working on is not going the way I want it to,**

A. I shrug it off because nothing is really that important.
B. I do something else and come back to the situation with a clear mind.
C. I mull over the problem but do my best to leave my worries at work.
D. I can't let it go. I worry to the point that it keeps me up at night.

11. **When it comes to paying the bills in our home,**

A. I don't have anything to do with it.
B. It doesn't matter who does it as long as it gets done.
C. I do it myself if time allows or review the job if it was done by someone else to be sure I know what's going on.
D. I always do it myself because I want to know exactly where our money is going, and I want to be sure the bills are paid on time.

12. I'm reading a book on being a control freak because

A. Someone gave it to me. I'm not sure why.

B. I am primarily concerned with finding ways to cope with the overcontrolling people around me. But if reading the book keeps me from being controlling, that's great too.

C. I know that I have controlling tendencies and hope the book might help me improve.

D. I read through a few parts I think are best—just to be in the know—and don't give much weight to ideas I disagree with.

Scoring. Give yourself one point for every A you circled, two for every B, three for every C, and four for every D. Use the following information to interpret your total score:

- *Score of 13 or fewer.* You aren't anywhere close to being a control freak. In fact, you may benefit from taking a course on assertiveness training.

- *Score of 14-22.* You are probably pretty easygoing and rarely battle the control freak within.

- *Score of 23-35.* You certainly have some control freak symptoms and can be diagnosed with occasional control freak flare-ups.

- *Score of 36-48.* It's undeniable. You have a full-blown case of control freak flu.

You may say, "O.K. So I do have a tendency to control, and I can see that this is not a good way to be. How can I go about changing myself?" The next chapter offers a suggestions.

Taming the Control Freak Within Us

F irst of all, if you have admitted that you are a controller, you have already taken a giant step toward making desirable changes in yourself. Most control freaks vehemently deny that there is anything wrong with their behavior and they have no desire whatever to change.

Most of our character traits are not of recent vintage. They have probably been with us since our early years. It stands to reason that they are not going to change overnight.

Many control freaks are what has been referred to as "Type A" personalities. These are people who are task-driven and operate under pressure of time constraints. They are often impatient both with themselves and others. They tend to hurry even when hurrying serves no purpose.

The "Type A" personality was actually discovered due to the astute observation made by an upholsterer. He was reupholstering the chairs in the waiting room of a heart specialist and remarked to the doctor, "It's a funny thing. All your chairs are worn out most at the front edge of the seat." This caught the doctor's attention, and he then noticed that most of his patients do not sit back on the chair, but rather sit on the front edge of the chair, ready to jump up at any moment. They do this even if they may be waiting for more than an hour for their appointment. He concluded that it is characteristic of people with heart disease to be on constant alert, ready to jump into action at a moment's notice. He reasoned that perhaps this attitude of constant readiness to jump into action may be a contributing factor to heart disease. This led him to study the personality traits of people with heart disease, and he came up with a profile of "Type A" people.

It is not wise nor even feasible to make a radical personality change. Rather, this can be accomplished very gradually, beginning with one feature of "Type A" or control freaks.

An example of the gradual process of change is that of a woman who replaced a shabby looking chair in her living room. But the new chair now made the old sofa look out of place, so she bought a new sofa. These two new pieces of furniture clashed with the carpet, so that was replaced. Now the drapes were out of sync with the rest of the room. Then the wallpaper and lamps had to be brought into harmony. The whole living room was ultimately totally changed, but it all began with the replacement of a single chair.

Much the same is true of character traits. There are some traits that are just incompatible with others. If we begin by working on a single trait, this may ultimately result in a major character change.

It is very common that controlling people are impatient and do not allow others to finish their sentences. They interrupt and finish the sentence for them. The Talmud says that a wise person will not interrupt another person's speech (*Ethics of the Fathers* 5:9).

This is a good starting point to begin to overcome controlling tendencies. Bite your lip if you have to, but do not finish other people's sentences for them. This takes a bit of effort, but you will be surprised how this can help you overcome impatience. Once you develop patience, you have taken a step toward divesting yourself of controlling.

Tone down your aggressiveness in driving. I know you are impatient because you are in a "no passing" zone and the driver in front of you is a slow poke. It has been shown that most often he will not delay you by more than two or three minutes. If you swing around and pass him, which is very risky in a "no passing" zone, you are likely to find that when you stop for a red light, he pulls up right behind you. You have gained only one car-length by passing him. If you can be more relaxed in driving, you have taken another step to overcome controlling.

Do you catch up on reading things pertaining to work during mealtime? Don't! Relax when you eat. Take this pressure off yourself. In general, do not do two things at the same time. If you are speaking with someone on the phone, it's O.K. to doodle, but do not rearrange your calendar or do arithmetical calculations.

Control and respect are antithetical. The greater the respect you have for a person, the less likely you are to control him. If a husband obeyed the Talmudic law to respect his wife even more than he respects himself, there would be no problem of wife abuse, which is, in the final analysis, an attempt to control. And if a person accorded others proper respect, as set forth in *Ethics of the Fathers* (2:15), there would be little control of others.

You will recall that we noted that the urge to control is often the result of low self-esteem. A person who feels inadequate and of low self-worth may resort to domineering others in order to compensate for his feelings of inferiority. Elevating one's self-esteem and gaining greater respect for oneself may eliminate the need to compensate by control. It would help to realize that exercising control over others is making the statement, "I don't think too much of myself."

Listening to others' opinions and judiciously deferring when appropriate is a statement of self-esteem. The Talmud says that an honorable person is one who accords honor to others (*Ethics of the Fathers* 4:1). Showing respect for others is, therefore, self-respect as well.

The Talmud states an important principle: "Just as it is a mitzvah to instruct someone if he will listen to you, it is also a mitzvah *not* to instruct someone if you know he will not listen to you" (*Yevamos* 65b). Control freaks often try to control the uncontrollable, whether people or things. This cannot but result in frustration.

Learn to speak softly, *especially* when you are angry. This is not so much in the interest of other people as it is in your own interest. When you shout or raise your voice, the other person tunes you out, and he does not hear what you are saying. In fact, he is defensively thinking how to respond to you. He is too occupied with his response to be able to take in what you are saying. If what you have to say has merit, say it softly. You will get your message across much more effectively.

A preacher left the text to his sermon on the lectern. Someone noticed that he had made notes in the margin to tell himself how to deliver the sermon. "Speak very slowly here," or "gesture with hands," or "pause for a moment." In one place the note read, "Argument awfully weak here. Yell very loud."

If your point is valid, do not shout. Yelling is a sign that your argument is weak.

Giving in to the urge to control is not much different than giving in to the urge to drink. You may get a brief "high," but no long-term gratification. People who have satisfaction in life don't need these artificial highs.

The Talmud says, "Who is a wealthy person? One who is satisfied with whatever one has" (*Ethics of the Fathers* 4:1). Our appetites may be insatiable, and if we feel we are missing out in life, we may seek other gratifications, whether alcohol, drugs, wealth, fame and yes, control. The happier you are with yourself, the less will be your need to control. Being content with what you have does not only deem you wealthy, but also eliminates many of the stresses that result from pursuit of ephemeral pleasures.

If you believe in G–d and that He has control of the world, your need to control others will diminish. One person wisely said, "I used to stay up nights worrying about things. Then I realized that G–d is always awake, so there's no use in both of us staying up. That enabled me to sleep more peacefully."

The Talmud says that G–d controls everything except for a person's ethical and moral behavior. Our own behavior, therefore, is what we must control, because G–d does not control it. Everything else may be left to His control.

Some people have an aversion to asking for help and accepting help when appropriate. They may see a request for help as yielding to someone else's control. That is a mistake. We all need help at one time or another. If we can accept help when this is appropriate, it may lessen our need to control.

Some people feel that things can get done properly only if they do it themselves. One of Charles Schulz's characters in the *Peanuts* comic strip is Lucy, an arrogant, loudmouthed control freak who is a know-it-all. In one cartoon strip, Lucy says, "Having examined my life and found it to be without flaw, I am going to hold a ceremony and give myself a medal. Then I will make a rousing acceptance speech and greet myself in the receiving line. When you're perfect, you have to do everything yourself." Lucy is not well liked by any of the other *Peanuts* characters. A control freak should realize that controlling behavior like Lucy's does not win friends.

The Talmud says that we should emulate G–d's attributes (*Shabbos* 133b). In the account of Creation, G–d says, "Let Us make man" (*Genesis* 1:26). Who is the "us" to whom G–d is referring? Rashi explains that G–d took counsel with the angels, not because He needed their advice, but to model for us and teach us that even the wisest person should seek advice from people of lesser wisdom.

G–d also models for us by delegating missions to angels. Have you ever wondered why G–d has angels carry out His wishes? G–d can do everything Himself. He is at all places at all times and is all-powerful. The reason G–d delegates to angels is, like His taking counsel with angels, to teach us that even the All-Perfect Being delegates. We should learn from this that we should delegate, regardless of how perfect we may think ourselves to be.

A parent asked me, "Is it right to apologize to my child and admit that what I did was wrong? Won't that diminish my authority over him?" I answered, "If you do not model apology and admission of a mistake, from where do you expect your child to learn it?" Apologizing and admitting one was wrong does not diminish one's authority. To the contrary, it earns the child's respect.

Control freaks find it difficult to admit they were wrong. By admitting a mistake, you will be overcoming controlling tendencies.

Controlling behavior is likely to elicit a controlling response. Parents who rule over their children with an iron hand often find that their children react by controlling them. And make no mistake about it: Kids know how to push their parents' buttons.

So take an honest look at yourself and see whether you have some control freak behavior. To the extent that you can eliminate it, you will be better liked by others, and you will like yourself much more too.

Epilogue

t has been said that those who do not learn from history are doomed to repeat it. This is obvious from the history of world conquests. Powerful leaders conquered countries and built empires, and the story is always the same. The glory of conquest, ruling the world, then disintegrating: Rome, Greece, Napoleon's France, the British Empire. Megalomania blinds one to the inevitable.

As in the macrocosm, so in the microcosm. There is a milder form of megalomania that drives individuals to seek to exert their power and authority over others. However, the rise and fall of individual power-seekers is not as evident as that of empire builders. The blindness to the futility of trying to dominate others is even greater in personal relationships than in world conquests.

Perhaps there is an inborn desire to exert power, but like many other traits, it must be properly channeled. The Talmud says, "Who is a mighty person? One who is master over his inclinations" (*Ethics of the Fathers* 4:1). In contrast to domination over others, self-mastery can be beneficial and enduring, but it requires much effort. The biographies of our great personalities testify that this can be achieved, but one must be willing to invest the effort.

The *tzaddik* of Apt said, "In my youth, I thought I would be able to change the world. As I grew older and wiser, I realized that this was impossible, but I thought I could change my community. I found that this, too, was impossible, but I was certain that I could change my family. Now I realize that it is all I can do to change myself."

I have tried to point out that control over others is both an illusion and counterproductive. Furthermore, as long as one discharges the urge for power by seeking to control others, one does not channel that urge to control oneself.

Why fail when you can succeed? Teach, inform and model behavior so that others will desire to emulate you and understand the propriety of your ways. This will make you happier and contribute to their well-being as well.